The Arbitrary Placement of Walls

The Arbitrary Placement *of* WALLS

Martha Soukup

DreamHaven

FIRST EDITION

ACKNOWLEDGEMENTS

"Dress Rehearsal", Originally published in *Universe 16*, Doubleday, Copyright © 1986 Martha Soukup

"Living in the Jungle", Originally published in *Writers of the Future Vol. III*, Bridge, Copyright © 1987 Martha Soukup

"The Big Wish", Originally published in *F&SF*, Copyright © 1987 Martha Soukup

"Having Keith", Originally published in *Asimov's*, Copyright © 1988 Davis Publications, Inc.

"Over The Long Haul", Originally published in *Amazing Stories*, Copyright © 1989 TSR, Inc.

"Dog's Life", Originally published in *Amazing Stories*, Copyright © 1991 TSR, Inc.

"The Arbitrary Placement of Walls", Originally published in *Asimov's*, Copyright © 1992 Davis Publications, Inc.

"Things Not Seen", Originally published in *Analog*, Copyright © 1992 Davis Publications, Inc. Later republished in *More Whatdunits*, DAW, 1993

"The Story So Far", Originally published in *Full Spectrum 4*, Bantam, Copyright © 1993 Martha Soukup

"The Spinner", Originally published in *Xanadu 2*, Tor, Copyright © 1994 Martha Soukup

"Good Girl, Bad Dog", Originally published in *Alternate Outlaws*, Tor, Copyright © 1994 Martha Soukup

"Absent Friends", Originally published in *Christmas Ghosts*, DAW, Copyright © 1993 Martha Soukup

"A Defense of the Social Contracts", Originally published in *Science Fiction Age*, Copyright © 1993 Martha Soukup

"Jones and the Stray", Originally published in *A Starfarer's Dozen*, Harcourt Brace, Copyright © 1995 Martha Soukup

"Fetish", Originally published in *Off Limits*, St. Martin's Press, Copyright © 1996 Martha Soukup

"Alita in the Air", Originally published in *A Nightmare's Dozen*, Harcourt Brace, Copyright © 1996 Martha Soukup

"To Destroy Rats", Originally published in *Twists of The Tale*, Dell, Copyright © 1996 Martha Soukup

Book Design by Robert T. Garcia/Garcia Publishing Services

Published by DreamHaven Books
912 West Lake St. Minneapolis, Minnesota 55408

Trade Paperback: ISBN 0-0-9630944-8-3
Hardcover: ISBN 0-9630944-9-1

PRINTED IN THE UNITED STATES OF AMERICA

10 9 8 7 6 5 4 3 2 1

Dedication

For everyone who's been kind, from Cally and Cassy, who wanted to hear my stories before anyone else did, all through and sorry all the names aren't here. Few people can keep writing without kindnesses. And mostly for Michael, best friend in a wacky world, without whom.

Contents

Introduction

There is a certain mystique surrounding Martha Soukup. You hear whispers of it at science fiction conventions, in the private parties professional writers attend: 'Martha Soukup said this' or 'Martha Soukup did that'—idle gossip and speculation for the most part, because her fellow writers want to know more about her.

–John Betancourt, *Rosemary's Brain*, Introduction.

by Neil Gaiman

There's a flurry in the bar – a convention's underway! –
And the people dash to panel, and to room
Where there's beer in every bathtub and the authors meet the fans
And they sign their books (with glee), or don't (with gloom).
But when authors get together on their own in some plush suite
And they drink the best champagne from glass and shoe-cup,
Then they talk of just one thing: not advances, nor their agents.
No, at parties, they just talk of Martha Soukup.

> Oh it's "Martha this" and "Martha that" and "Martha Soukup said,"
> If you cannot talk of Martha then you might as well be dead.

On the chilly arctic plains when the winter night draws in
– The night that lasts for nearly bloody ever –
Then the fishermen and -ladies huddle fifty to a room
Round a fire, chew some blubber, and endeavour
To converse of matters rowdy, like the time Mung lost his hand,
Or the time the baby fell into the glue-cup.
But they fail. And for months they talk of nothing but Herself:
While the snows descend they talk of Martha Soukup.

Oh it's "Martha that" and "Martha this" and "Martha Soukup
  heard . . ."
If you cannot talk of Martha then you shouldn't say a word.

There are mountains in Tibet where the lamas pray and wait
In their monasteries lonely and forgot,
Where they levitate and fast and they recall the distant past
And do other wondrous things (don't ask me what).
And the holiest and oldest of these meditating men
Does not speak or sleep or eat or even puke-up,
But when his silence ends, so the wisest lamas claim,
It will only be to talk of Martha Soukup

Oh it's "Martha that" and "Martha this" and "Martha such and
  such . . ."
If you do not talk of Martha then you must be out of touch

At October's chilly end, when the leaves turn brown and red,
Then the vampires and zombies and the weird
Lurch and flutter from their graves to party down and party hard,
Dance or shamble, stuff their faces, and be cheered.
But when the ghouls get maudlin, and the phantoms start to pall,
Or they need to cheer the saddest little spook up,
The undead and the fearsome do not talk of blood or gore.
In sepulchral tones they talk of Martha Soukup.

Oh it's "Martha this" and "Martha that" and "Martha Soukup
  wrote . . ."
If you cannot talk of Martha you should better cut your throat.

Far beyond the Milky Way there are beings made of glass
Who have been observing us for many years.
They have classified our culture with their crystalline machines
(For they classify each race as it appears).
Our poets are inferior to the star-whale's lonely songs,
And they think our science more or less a fluke. Up
There, yes, they're hard to please, but there's one Earth thing they like
Telepathically they talk of Martha Soukup.

Oh it's "Martha this" and "Martha that" and "Martha, I
    beseech . . ."
If you do not talk of Martha what's the good of having speech?

In the rain forest, the bush, in the tundra or the kush,
The Sahara, the Sargasso, or the veldt,
There's a hundred thousand tribes with just one thing on their mind:
What she did and said and knew and thought and felt.
She's the Empress of their India, the apple of their eye,
And they tell her tales from Singapore to *soukh*. Yup,
Her name is what they trust, oft misspelled and oft discussed,
Let us join with them to talk of Martha Soukup.

So it's "Martha this" and "Martha that" and "Martha Soukup's
    tops,"
But you must have got the point by now, so this is where it stops.

Foreword

Writers are best off not talking much about their stories, unless they're geniuses or they don't mind looking silly, or both. (Both is nice.) On the other hand, I've always liked looking at story collections and seeing what writers thought they were up to.

So this is a compromise. Take a deep breath and read it all at once:

"Dress Rehearsal" is the first story I wrote after two tries in public school which were bounced by *F&SF*, after which I'd stopped for a decade. I wrote it as a sketch for my theater troupe Moebius Theatre, and then I wrote it as a story, trying too hard and putting too many words in it. At Clarion one professional writer told me it wasn't a seven-point story, and two others told me not to listen to that advice, so I sold it to Terry Carr, which was close enough to a dream that I'm probably not allowed any others.

"Living in the Jungle" was the third story I wrote since high school, and the second didn't count. I wrote it because I was reading a Joe Haldeman book and wanted something exciting to happen. Lizzy Lynn told me it needed a gun. "The Big Wish" isn't my first wish-fulfillment gone wrong story, "Dress Rehearsal" was, and I'd had that wish longer. "Having Keith" is because, among other things, horror stories don't always stop to think what things would really feel like.

"Over the Long Haul" is A.J. Budrys's truck but my everything else. Years later, Danny Glover filmed it as a 35-minute short called "Override" for Showtime. He lives in San Francisco too, but I still haven't met Danny Glover. "Dog's Life" confused a workshop of writers I visited who thought it was hard science fiction.

"The Arbitrary Placement of Walls" is settling, finally, into knowing what I'm doing, I think. "Things Not Seen" was written for a Mike Resnick book in which he supplied mystery gimmicks and his writers turned them inside out. I looked at it when I finished turning the gimmick inside out and decided it was proof I really could write hard science fiction, so there, so I had it published in *Analog* first and was awarded an "Analog Mafia" button.

"The Story So Far" is my Carol Emshwiller story, because it would be nice to be Carol Emshwiller when I grow up, but I don't know if anyone else can tell. It's from a line that came into my head as I woke up once that turned into a story, as "Fetish" later on was from a line that came into my head as I was falling asleep.

"The Spinner" is the story I was trying to write when I wrote "A Defense of the Social Contracts", but when I made it science fiction, it "Social Contracts" went off and became a story about its own things, so I tried again as a fairy tale. I sold "The Spinner" to Jane Yolen, because she knows fairy tales and I knew she'd help me get it right. I put foodstuffs and clothing into "Social Contracts" on purpose, and I sold it to Scott Edelman, because he's rather odd.

"Absent Friends" is set in my current apartment if you cut a room off one end, but I don't know any of those guys. "Jones and the Stray" and "Alita in the Air" came after years of fretting because Michael Stearns was sure I could write stories for kids, or young teenagers, and I wasn't sure. But I convinced myself, so he won the bet. "To Destroy Rats" is what happens when one's asked to write a cat story and one doesn't want to write about cats particularly (I know there are three different dog stories in this book, but actually two cats are what I have), and one realizes one has never written a Poe story.

That's everything you need to know about these stories. Anything else you believe about them is right. Anything you decide about me is as true as anything you decide about anyone else you haven't met, and I don't have a problem with it.

The Arbitrary Placement of Walls

Dress Rehearsal

Every note he whistled made his hangover worse, but Tom didn't mind the pain one bit. He refused to. He had earned this hangover, and he savored the memories that went with it.

He whistled off-key but with gusto, his head throbbing a stacatto counterpoint as he strode down the sidewalk; he followed the path cut by his whistled tune through the gray morning air, up to the steps of the theater.

The lock on the door stymied him briefly–the producer kept changing which finger's print opened the lock, in an attempt to improve security–but after a fumbled process of elimination Tom got the door open. He smiled at it and let his whistle carry him through the narrow doorway, through the dark lobby and into the murky, echoing theater. Working more from memory than sight, Tom swung down the left aisle, around dusty black curtains, past two motionless figures slumped in old reupholstered chairs, backstage and nearly smack into pacing, frowning Carl Waterbury.

"Morning," said Tom. The sudden stop had cost him balance. Perhaps last night's drinks weren't as finished with him as he had thought. "Whoa–awfully early out this morning, isn't it?"

"You're ten minutes late!" snapped Carl, thrusting his wrist under Tom's nose. The numbers on Carl's skin wouldn't quite come into focus.

"When you've been partying until four, any time is too early," Tom said amiably, pushing Carl's hand away. "I feel a great sense of accomplishment just being here at all."

Carl glared at him. "You know we open tomorrow."

"Sure I do. That's why I was partying until four," Tom said. "Everyone was there but you."

"We're hardly ready to celebrate yet!"

Carl was shorter than Tom, and stockier; he kept his hair trimmed tidily and unfashionably short, combed very neatly, while Tom's fine, no-color hair flopped every which way. Tom was no slob, but he could never see spending all that effort on physical appearance when he was just going to put on a costume anyway. Still, he knew Carl was judging his early morning dishevelment as unprofessional.

"Everyone at the party seemed to think we were," Tom said cheerfully.

Carl pressed his lips together, making an obvious effort to be calm. "At least Ed should have known that we haven't had a single blessed run of scene five properly and in costume, and we're not ready to do it in front of an audience!"

Tom winced. "All right, all right, hold your head on."

"Hat," snapped Carl.

"No, head." He grinned. "When you've been partying till four, it's most definitely hold your head on."

Carl sighed. "Whatever. Could we just get this scene down, please?"

After working with the man on and off for years, Tom still could not figure out where Carl had mislaid his sense of humor. "Okay, okay, you don't have to tell me more than twelve times." He flung his arms wide in an expansive gesture of brotherly love, then clasped Carl around the shoulders. "You got me!" he cried. "I'm here, I'm ready to work, I'm all yours!"

"Fine," said Carl. He peeled Tom's arm from its chummy embrace. "I'm sorry if I'm a little keyed up." He gestured at the silent figures on the stage. "With my costume down for repairs all week, this show of all shows—"

"You'll be swell. Nothing to worry about."

"This is a new kind of role for me. I've only been in costume for ten minutes since the auditions. We can run our lines a thousand times—but until I can do the key scene in costume, I have no idea if it's going to work." Carl kneaded nervously at his neck.

Tom felt a warm twinge of empathy; no wonder the guy was a basket case. Being cast against type was exciting, an actor's dream; it was sometimes an actor's nightmare as well. It was not easy to go on a blinding stage and draw from yourself an entirely alien character. Still, Carl's part was a small one, what Ed, the director, had called a "featured role," no *tour de force* part.

"Sure it'll work. You're a pro," Tom said reassuringly, but Carl did not look reassured. "Hey! Remember when you played the four-year-old in 'Attic Games'? You did great. You got so far into the part on opening night, you bit my costume on the nose! I swear I was in pain all the way in the control chair."

Carl smiled faintly for the first time. Of course it was impossible to feel pain, or one's own body, when in costume.

"You deserved it, you know," he said. "Your part may have called for brattiness, but you took it above and beyond the call of duty."

"Sheer creative genius," Tom said loftily, with a broad, theatrical gesture. "I suffer for my art." Now that it seemed Carl had thawed, he walked over to the main control board—which theater people, traditionalists, still called it, although these days it was only a nondescript panel on a small, dusty box—and flicked on the power switches for their costumes. Only a member of the stage technician's union was supposed to touch the boards, but the techs usually winked at small touch-up rehearsals. Carl had already powered up the main circuits.

Carl grunted, moody again. So much for cheering him up; but such a small part to get worked up over! His character was only in a flashback or two for Tom's character, Kevin. Perhaps that was it, jealousy over stage time. Couldn't blame an ambitious actor for that.

"You know it'll look great on your resume," Tom reminded Carl as he took his place in his control chair, checking to make sure each strap was secure. "Directors are always looking for versatility. One good notice to quote and you'll impress the hell out of them."

"Sure," Carl said abstractedly, stealing a final glance at the figures on stage as he fixed the projection band carefully around his forehead. He slipped his wrists into their constraints on the chair's arms and pressed the left button to close them. He looked across at Tom. "Ready?"

"Fastest prep in the Midwest," replied Tom. "Go!"

Both actors pressed their right-hand buttons.

○ ○ ○

The transfer always hit Tom as a swirl of vertigo, lit by the dazzling, black-on-black spirals he sometimes saw when, tired, he stood too fast. Other actors had confided to Tom that in that instant they felt out of control, vulnerable; Tom preferred to think of it as the nearest thing to spaceflight that anyone in his currently Earth-bound profession could experience. In that moment lay the freedom to become anyone at all, more fully than any previous generation of actors could have known, and Tom spent the whole glorious flight savoring that thrill.

None of this impressed the engineers who had created costume technology. They would point out that the transfer of perception occurred at the speed of light: transferring across a room was an experience too brief to notice. The feeling of motion and any other sensory impressions that accompanied it were concoctions of the brain adapting to the sudden change. No matter. Whatever Tom felt was real enough for him.

All perception of Tom's own body disappeared as he entered the Kevin costume. When the room settled, he stretched Kevin's arms up, down and behind his back, testing out the costume and enjoying his favorite side effect of the transference.

"Isn't it great the way the hangover disappears when you go into costume? I love show business!" The voice still sounded strange to his ears, more tenor than his own. He had come to this play off a string of heavies with much deeper voices, and the older Kevin costume in which he spent most of the play had a rawer, throatier voice.

There was no answer. He looked around and saw that Carl had already stood his costume up and was pacing Sarah experimentally across the narrow stage, moving the joints gingerly, one at a time.

"It looks like they finally got all the bugs out of her," Carl said with Sarah's voice, a pleasant, slightly raspy soprano that did not fit well with Carl's gruff tone.

"All the money they charge to rent these things, there shouldn't be any bugs in the first place," Tom commented. He unfastened the restraining strap, tucked it behind the chair's cushion, and stood, watching the other costume with amusement. It was of a young woman in her late twenties (about Carl's age, so no stretch there), slender and attractive with a dimple beside the chin and a slightly upturned nose, charmingly dressed in a long, clingy blue business dress of ten years before. The effect was ruined by the tentative, mechanical way Carl moved her as he tested the costume's responses, and his obvious difficulty in balancing with the topless, suction high-heeled shoes.

"How does it look to you?" asked the Sarah costume, pirouetting stiffly and experimentally. Its left shoe popped up. With a quick and entirely natural movement, the costume grabbed it, sat on a chair's arm and tried to plaster it back onto the foot.

Tom couldn't help himself. With Kevin's most wolflike leer, he purred, "You look ravishing, sweetheart."

"Oh, cut it out, Tom." The soprano voice was irritated; the shoe would not stay on.

Tom crossed his costume to Sarah, took the shoe. "Playing hard to get, hmmm?" he teased. The costume grabbed for the shoe. He laughed and held it out of reach. "You know you can trust *me*, baby."

"*Tom!*" Sarah's face was made for glaring, with a ridiculously beautiful-when-angry look, even funnier when you remembered that it was only Carl Waterbury.

"What's the matter, darling, wrong time of the month?"

"Tom!" The costume leapt to its feet. The other shoe came off. It stumbled back against the chair and stood there glowering, lips pressed together, breathing heavily—obviously in anger, not shortness of breath. The costumes did not need to breathe. "Not funny!"

"I'm sorry," said Tom, abashed. "It was just a joke."

"Some sense of humor." Tom was silent. "I didn't even want this part to start out with! It was Ed's idea to cast the play experimentally. But I'm stuck with it now and the least you can do is not make it any harder than it already is!"

"I'm sorry," Tom said again. He should have known Carl wouldn't think it was funny. He held out the shoe, a peace offering. "Here."

"Thanks." The Sarah costume had relaxed its posture, but the lips were still compressed, and it didn't meet Tom's eyes.

"Look, I was a jerk. Sometimes I don't know when to stop." He watched the shoe turn in Sarah's soft plastic hand. "You've got to walk real steady in those, keep your feet pressed down firmly. Girlfriend told me that."

"Right."

"Actually, you might as well not even wear them for now. They're not really designed to adhere to plastic. The props master can probably glue them or rivet them or something later."

"But then I'll be rehearsing at the wrong height—oh, whatever. Let's just get this scene down, all right? If it looks good after the first one or two runs we'll have an hour for breakfast before the rest of the cast arrives, and I won't have to worry about the damn thing anymore."

"Sure," Tom said. "Need a script?"

"I should hope not! I've been over these lines a hundred times. Just because I don't have my costume doesn't mean I'm not working."

Nobody said you weren't, Tom thought. Aloud he said, "Fine. You enter stage left, I'm reading the sports." As the other padded offstage in stocking feet, he adjusted the angles of the armchairs and picked up a thin sheaf of hardcopy from the square coffee table between them. He settled into his armchair, crossed his legs, spread the hardcopy on one thigh, and took in a deep, focusing breath.

Ten years earlier. Establishing the roots of Kevin's character. Childish, manipulative, he tries to take the upper hand over the woman who is leaving him. Yet he does still care for her, and she still for him, although both are too vulnerable to admit it. Probably his last chance to open himself up to her, or anyone.

He let out the breath. "Lights up," he called.

Enter Sarah, stage left, forcefully. She threw her heavy purse on the coffee table with a crash and glared down at him. That was his cue. He didn't look up from the sports finals.

"Oh, it's you," he said, jotting notes on the baseball tables.

In Sarah's sweet, harsh voice: "Damn right it is!"

He continued his notations, said casually, "I'd have thought you'd be in Oregon by now."

"So would I!"

With elaborate casualness: "Then you changed your mind?"

Half an octave higher: "Changed my mind?" A deep breath, then lower, seething: "*Nothing* could make me change my mind."

He looked up at her, head tilted in a sincere pose. "But you've come back to me," he said logically.

"Oh. Yes. Because when I reached the shuttle, I found out *someone* had cancelled the charge on my ticket!"

"Oh my," he said mildly.

"And then I found out that *someone* had removed my charge plate from my purse!"

"You don't say."

"And *someone* invalidated my emergency cash access code!"

He smirked. "Who could have done that?"

"You monster!"

My god, Carl's actually jumped a cue, he thought with mild surprise; but he could cover and they'd fix it on the next run.

She rubbed fiercely at her neck and continued the premature line. "You manipulative bastard! Why can't you just get out of my life, damn it?" She was leaning over him, barefoot, flushed, simulated blood raising color high in her cheeks, her eyes flashing. Here was where Kevin would feel triumph at getting a rise out of her.

He threw back his head and laughed.

Before he could react, she cursed and brought a hand sharply across his cheek.

He didn't feel it as a sting, but the costume relayed the force of the impact to his brain; she had hit hard. He was bewildered. This had nothing to do with the script. He shook his head and looked up. A look of triumph was on her face, and her hand was pulled back for another blow. He stood, pushing the armchair back with the force of his movement, and grabbed her by the wrist. She hit him with her other hand.

"Hey there—" he burst out as he grabbed her left wrist, wrenching her around tight against his left side. Her soft silicone breasts compressed against him. She struggled to release herself; he twisted her arms to keep the leverage. Her face was inches beneath his, and he could see fury and perhaps hatred lighting up her eyes, her mouth working, red and twisted. He held her closely, confused, not knowing what she might do. She spat in his face.

He didn't think. He immobilized her face with his, crushing her mouth beneath his mouth. She made an angry, strangled squeak of outrage and hit him glancingly with her knee, so that he had to pin her legs between him and the coffee table. His sensors told him that she tried to bite his lip, but failed to get a good purchase; then they registered a gradual softening of her mouth. His head buzzed strangely. He released her wrists, slipped his arms behind her and up and under the jacket of her business dress, up to the skin over the smooth mechanisms of her shoulders. He kissed her. She sank gently to sit on the table, not moving to hold him but not resisting, eyes closed.

Suddenly uncomfortable, he broke away. She did not look at him as he took a step back and stared down at her.

"Sarah," he said.

She groped behind her, located the purse by the edge of the table and clutched it to her. She stood clumsily, as though still wearing the unaccustomed shoes. "I'll—I'll be staying with Francie until I get my code reinstated," the costume said, still not meeting his eyes.

She's gone back to the script, he thought numbly. "I'll visit you there," said Tom, awkwardly.

"No! No. Don't—Kevin. I won't let you see me."

"You can't stop me," he said, but she had already turned away and was fleeing the stage. The prop door closed behind her. There was nothing behind the door but a closet-sized space; he stared at it for several long moments before it burst open and Carl's costume emerged, walking briskly toward the armchairs.

"I guess I'll get that breakfast now," the Sarah costume said brightly, settling into a chair and putting on the shoulder strap.

"The scene wasn't supposed to end there," said Tom.

"It worked, didn't it?" He said nothing as she flicked the little switch beneath her wrist. She slumped slightly before the costume's automatic controls switched on, keeping it in a seated position. He looked down at the lifeless mannequin.

"You're the one who wanted to work!" he told it.

From behind him came the sharp clicks of constraints snapping open. "I'll tell Ed we improvised a better ending, all right?" said Carl. Tom whirled to face the voice. Carl was making a quick exit down through the empty audience.

"No!" said Tom, leaping down from the stage. By hurdling two seats, he was able to block Carl before Carl could reach the lobby. Carl tried to duck around him. He grabbed the actor's wrist.

"Tom, let go of me!"

"Something happened up there. We have to talk."

"Nothing happened," Carl grunted angrily, trying to wrench loose. Metal and plastic were stronger than muscle and bone. "Don't be an idiot!" Stocky, hard-featured, he could not have looked less like

Sarah, and Tom suddenly felt like an idiot indeed. Any actor knew that what was done on stage was not always a reflection of the performer. Tom was sure he was nothing like Kevin.

"Carl," he started, not knowing what he wanted to say.

"It's the costume up there! It's cute, you've got a crush on it. Now let go of me!"

"Not until we talk," Tom insisted. He tightened his grip on Carl's wrist. If Carl was this upset, Tom was determined to make him face up to whatever had happened.

"You maniac—let go of me—" Carl struggled helplessly to free himself. Suddenly he smashed his free hand across the costume's plastic and metal face.

At Carl's surprised cry of pain, Tom almost let go. He looked at Carl and suddenly saw Sarah, the frightened fury burning in the eyes, the high spots of color in the face, desperate emotion and humiliation. He saw a fierce and vulnerable and weirdly endearing person, something he had never seen in Carl before.

As Tom blinked at this double vision, Carl twisted his hand around and managed to jostle the switch below his costume's wrist. The last thing he heard was Carl's grunt of victory.

The room swirled black and fell away beneath him.

"Carl?" called Tom. He opened his eyes and sat up, then moaned as newly-remembered pain pounded in his head. "Where did—that was cheap, Carl."

He hit the button that released his constraints, yanked the band from his head and stood up. The room started to go black again.

Tom steadied himself and walked out to the stage. He could see his costume standing lopsidedly near the lobby door. Automatically he went to retrieve it, walking it carefully back up to the stage and over to its chair, seating Kevin mannequin once again beside Sarah mannequin.

He looked at the female figure. It was very attractively built. Could he just have been reacting to its manmade charms? Tom was beginning to doubt everything that had happened that morning.

"All right, we'll see," he muttered.

He knelt like a suitor before her, looking up at her slack face with its dark hair falling across one cheek. He put one hand on either side of her slender waist and stood, raising her to her feet.

"What do you say, Sarah?" he asked softly. He took her gently by the chin, raised her pale face up to his. Ten months before he had played Bassanio to the same costume's Portia; a pleasant middle-aged actress had operated the costume. Sarah's open eyes stared blankly at him.

He kissed her.

The soft plastic lips lay quietly beneath his. The dark green eyes seemed flat, opaque. Mysterious, but trivial. Sarah was just a machine. Tom smiled sadly and lowered the costume back to its seat. He knew with sudden certainty that he would never see Carl again when the show was over.

"But it wasn't the goddamn costume," he said. One high-heeled shoe lay beside him. He picked it up. "Carl!" he shouted at the lobby door, and grimaced in agony. The name echoed throbbing in his head, blotting out the world.

"Jeez, what a hangover," muttered Tom. "I hate show business." He dropped the shoe and walked alone from the theater.

Living in the Jungle

I don't want to leave the Jungle.

They're trying to take me out, of course. Just this morning, before dawn, they sent in another robot. It was the kind that's slung very low and articulated into twenty sections, each with a separate tread and retractable legs. I took it out with a coconut. If you sneak up alongside them it takes three or four seconds for them to sense you, and while the front sensory segment is whipping around to get a fix on you you can take the half shell in each hand and scoop them in and under the oval front plate. The milky meat provides just enough lubrication. There's a lot of resistance when the shell meets the cabling, but you don't have to break it completely—something in there is fragile enough to make its input go blooey. That's the start.

Then the rear end starts to whip around to get a fix on you instead, and its sensors won't tumble to the coconut system because they're on a flush immobile seamless panel, but on the other hand they're not so sensitive either. A handful of mud smeared across the plate will slow it down. Then while the thing starts to thrash a little you can give it enough of a kick to make it go belly-up. There's a lot of stuff down there, when you loosen the thumbscrews, that you can disable with your hands even. A heavy stick is better. The whole thing takes maybe thirty seconds and then you've got a dead robot.

I don't know very much about robots or most machines, so while learning this I scarred up my ribcage pretty badly and broke two fingers on my left hand, tore out a huge patch of hair and took some other minor damage. I suppose it's something I should've studied up on first. But I'll tell you that now there isn't anyone who knows so much about how to destroy something she understands so little.

o o o

"Whatcha doing, honey?"

She looked up, startled. She was reading, slowly and carefully, trying to figure out if Hegel was really an idiot or if perhaps she was.

The man was dressed like a jock, sweatshirt over a one-piece jogging suit, with incredibly new sports shoes. The baggy shirt didn't quite hide the fact that he was losing the figure of a jock. He was a complete stranger. She shook her head a little, trying to come into the real world.

"A quiet one, huh?" The book was snatched from her hands. "Whoa! Lookit this. Hegel!" He pronounced it Hee-gull. He mimed a great strain on his arm. "Awful heavy stuff for such a little girl." He winked at her. "Do you know what it's about?"

"Well," she began, "I don't know—"

"I didn't think so," he said. "A cute little thing like you."

When the robot had stopped twitching and I'd ripped out everything rippable and twisted and bent everything that wasn't, I went over it thoroughly. A lens out of the front section can start a fire by focusing sunlight on dead leaves; the last one I was using I managed to drop in the river. There was no finding it in all those rocks and mud. An edge of the legs can be pried off to make a good skewer and a fair knife. They don't last long so I always need more.

The power supply is something I like to take, although I've had no idea what I'll do with them. They make an artistic stack in the corner of my lean-to. Wires are good for tying fowl while I'm cooking it, for holding my lean-to together, for holding my hair back in a ragged tail, for making traps, for a million things. There are only a few long useful pieces. I wrenched out those I could, braided them together, and strung it all through a loop of my pants. The pants are getting ragged, and I'll have to think about what to do when they wear out: they were my third and last pair. Everything else I bundled in a wrapping of banana leaves to take home with me.

Killing a robot is like a day at the market.

The groceries were too heavy to hold in one arm, and it had been a morning decreed for rain, making the ground too wet to set them down. She grunted the bags to one side, freeing one thumb and fore-finger to work the latch. She got the door open, then turned quickly to hold it open with her back.

As she was backing into the lobby against the heavy door, it was pulled away from behind her. Clutching the bags, she toppled into the building and banged her head on the old tile floor.

The matronly woman holding the door above her looked cha-grinned. Then she pulled her face into a stern mother's expression.

"You should have your groceries delivered like a normal person," she scolded. "You see what happens?"

The Jungle isn't much, I suppose. I always used to picture long constricting snakes hanging from every tree and huge bands of mon-keys and apes clambering in the trees with them, and lions staring up at you and leopards staring down at you with cool murder in their faces, and more kinds of giant insects than you could count in a year, and mongooses and parrots and elephants—killing and dying all the time, all making this wild musical shriek of noise all through the day and the night.

I don't know where I got it from—maybe an old Tarzan sound-track—but the noise was the best part of the image. The jungles I imagined were places for whooping and shrieking. This Jungle is very quiet, and the few animals here seem to keep their thoughts to themselves.

By the time I finished scavenging the robot, the sun had begun to light things up some. I left its shell, littered with the bits and pieces I didn't think I'd need, and started back to my lean-to.

The beginning of the day is the best time to look at the Jungle, which is why I was up before dawn to start out with. When it's just getting light you can't tell the difference between the little, real trees, and the big, synthetic ones that loom overhead. They made a small effort to make the big temporaries look real, but it doesn't stand up to full daylight.

In silhouette, though, they loom over my head as alive as any ghosts. Real vines dangle down from their plastete branches, and an occasional real parakeet or finch flits from limb to limb, not caring that they're not nature's own perches. Nor would the birds, seeing as they're such live-for-today types, care that the trees are designed to disintegrate over the next couple of decades, as the real trees grow up to replace them.

Nor do I care, as long as they're here for me now.

"You work in the government," she pleaded. "You could have them change this." She shook the letter at Marie like a cat trying to stun a mouse.

"I'm sorry, honey," her older sister said. "It's not my place to do that."

"But they want to take away my car!"

"And give you a better one," Marie said reasonably.

"And give me one that drives itself!"

"Most people like them. It gives you a chance to relax, read, watch some television. Is that so bad?"

"I like driving myself."

"Then you ought to have been more careful. If you hadn't broken traffic laws they wouldn't be making you trade in your old car towards a computer-driven one."

"Then you aren't going to help me fight this?"

Marie sighed. "Nikkie, as far as I'm concerned, they were right when they had the original idea of just impounding violators' cars. I have a little boy. I don't want some dangerous driver threatening his life on the road when a computer can do it so much better." The younger woman would have smiled, if she hadn't been so upset.

Marie tousled her sister's hair, as she had when they were small. "Cheer up! It's not the end of the world."

She watched Marie let herself out the front door, shook open the letter. It listed her lifetime infractions at the bottom: Running four red lights. Speeding, once, in Wisconsin. A broken taillight. A missing muffler. Some parking tickets.

Eyes stinging, she crumpled up the notice and flung it at the wall.

I strolled back to my lean-to and got another surprise. It was collapsing.

I went through weeks of experimentation before I even found a shelter I liked. I didn't bring very much stuff with me—after all, I was only supposed to be a tourist and I was supposed to be staying in civilization—and, like a lot of things, I just hadn't thought through the living arrangement question.

I had brought, because they seemed vaguely useful and important, two clear plastic tarps.

The first night I was here, I ended up wrapping myself in one of the tarps, like it was a big plastic sleeping bag. The odds and ends I brought with me, which I also thought would be important and useful, I wrapped in the other. I used the lumpy second tarp as a pillow. There I camped, under the sky and everything.

In the middle of the night I woke up shouting from a vivid nightmare. I'd been naked and tied down in a steambath, and the attendant kept hitting me with wet towels that were covered with little stingers. It was a relief, for two seconds, to open my eyes to darkness and not that horrible place.

Then I discovered I was still in that horrible place.

I was drenched in sweat from being wrapped in plastic. Better yet, I'd put myself right in the path of a colony of ants. I wasn't so tightly wrapped up that they couldn't find their way into my tarp, which is exactly what they did. As I've come to learn, nothing will stop a bunch of ants from being exactly where they want to be, and where they wanted to be was where I was. And since I was there, well hell, they might as well give me a taste. Or some good healthy stings to show they didn't appreciate me rolling over and crushing the life out of them.

It's very hard to get out of plastic mummy-wrappings when you're screaming, soaking, in pain and in panic. But I'll bet I looked funny.

I broke a bunch of the stuff I'd wrapped in my pillow. (Just as well—what did I really need my alarm clock for? I don't even use my little pinkie watch anymore. And shampoo I'd have had to learn to live without eventually. I wish the bottle hadn't broken, though. I was eating shampoo-flavored dried food and vitamin pills for weeks.)

That very day I started to devote serious attention to How to Build a Better Shelter.

It took, if I'm counting right, seventeen separate attempts before I got it the way I wanted it. Of course, the later incarnations were perfectionist fiddling. Only the first six or seven were complete flops, no better than sleeping out in the rain.

Not terribly far from my favorite river there were three plastete trees all in a row, pretty close together. Vines hung down between them. I ended up weaving leaves through the vines to fill in the gaps, a two-day project that resulted in a nicely wind- and rainproof wall. Then, climbing the trees a little (*that's* not easy; you can pull yourself up on the vines just fine, but that rough plastete scrapes your skin raw), I attached a tarp to one end of my tree-and-vine wall, then to the other. The front I tacked to the ground.

Vines make mediocre ropes for tying that sort of thing, but by that time I'd experienced the thrill of my first robot kill. I'd just wanted to get as far from its body as possible after it happened, and it took me hours to relocate it, but the image of its wires and cables kept me looking. I was learning.

Ten modifications later, after I finished rigging up a floor from bamboo slats on stones—keeps some of the insects from walking across your bed—I was just getting happy with my little home. But now I came into my clearing and found the right-hand tree was disintegrating.

I set everything down carefully before panicking. Then I ran full tilt to the lean-to.

He stepped forward and neatly blocked her way. He wore a button that said "GIVE" in tasteful simulated wood. She avoided looking at him and tried to sidestep him, but somehow he had already guided her behind a table of leaflets.

"I know what you're thinking," he said. "Another dumb charity drive, and probably one you don't even support." She looked up into a broad, smiling face. "I can understand that reaction. So many good causes. So hard to choose between them. And so many of them just fall by the wayside, because nobody can spend all the time it would take to learn how to do the good they want to do. Leaving you feeling guilty about the good not done.

"And you do want to do good, don't you?" He paused, waiting for her response. She stared at him. "Of course you do. We all do.

"That's what GIVE is for. All we ask you to do is fill out one questionnaire. We take a complete psychological profile of you, we find out exactly what your own individual values are.

"And from then on, you have nothing to worry about! Your profile tells us what you want to give to each cause. Abused children, homeless kittens, the lunar station, your church of choice, the gun lobby—they'll all get the fraction of your donation that your profile dictates. So if you'll just sign up now, we can run you through right away."

She shook her head.

"No time now? Give me your number and we'll call to work out an appointment." He smiled at her. He was sincere, concerned.

She turned and walked away.

"Would you care to leave a general donation to GIVE?" he called after her.

She tipped the table of leaflets as she passed.

The right-hand tree was indeed crumbling. Worse, it was collapsing toward the lean-to. For a moment I wondered if the tarp was heavy enough to pull the tree down.

Of course that couldn't be the case. So I calmed myself down and walked around the tree to get a better look at it.

It was coming down, losing its structure around the base. It looked like it was being eaten away from the inside. They were supposed to do that eventually, but this just had to be too early. I rapped my hand against it a few times, trying to decide if it was still sturdy enough to risk going inside. I decided to go inside anyway.

I had to keep punching the ceiling up out of my face, and finally I just stuck both hands up and held it off. It was a mess inside. All of my somewhat arranged piles of things were knocked askew by the collapsing plastic that draped over everything.

If I couldn't predict when the trees were going to wear out, how was I going to manage a stable home?

I went back outside and shoved the plastic under the floor stones on the right-hand side, straightening out the shelter's wall as much as possible. Then I took another look inside.

My pile of power packs had been directly in front of the falling tree, and had been knocked all over the floor by it. I vaguely remembered moving them before I went out, after I tripped on them trying to get to the door flap.

I shoved them back and started to pick up the rest of the stuff on the floor.

Something seemed off. I looked back and I could actually see the tree bending in toward me—

"Holy shit, the batteries!" I screamed. Don't ask me who else was around to care. I cared enough for triplets. Between the contacts of a couple power packs, where they touched the tree, the plastete was eroding merrily away.

I thought of moving the power packs, but decided it was the better part of valor to hit the floor—the left-hand side of the floor.

The tarp came crashing down around me.

She was curled on the sofa in his living room, her chin on her knee, watching him. He paced around the room.

"For God's sake, Nikkie," he said. "You quit your job?"

"It didn't mean anything."

"What the hell do you mean, it didn't mean anything? Do you really want to live on the dole level? Do you have something against eating well?"

She frowned and said nothing.

"I mean, if you need some help from me, okay. You can move in here—I've been asking you to do that anyway, if you'd only listen to good ideas for once—but it's just stupid to give up your paycheck." He stopped pacing, stood over her and shook his head. "Jesus. It's not like shuffling papers for six hours a day is going to kill you or anything. Everyone else does it."

"I'm not everyone else," she said, very quietly.

"Most people really *like* a little bit of security. It's no skin off your nose to follow the rules once in a while."

Her hand clenched at a sofa cushion. "I'm not most people."

"You're obviously just going to keep acting like a child—"

"I'm not a child!" she shouted. She wrenched up the sofa cushion and flung it at the wall. It didn't help. "I am not a fucking child and I don't have to be taken care of! If people would just leave me alone once I might even be able to accomplish something for a change!"

"Jesus, Nikkie!" He stared at her, uncomprehending. "What are you so hostile about all of a sudden? It's not like anyone's stopping you from doing anything. Stop being so paranoid, for Christ's sake."

She was on her feet. Every muscle in her body was knotted. It felt like every muscle had been knotted for years.

"Shit, you never even swear," he said. "I don't know what's wrong with you today."

"I guess you don't," she said. She went to the door. She took a deep breath, then turned to face him. Her voice was almost steady. "Why don't you just stop worrying about it? I doubt I'm worth your valuable concern."

The door slammed behind her.

My first impulse was to slash my way free with the dagger in my boot, but then I wouldn't have the tarp anymore. I freed my face before my lungs burst and freed the rest of my body in good time. I didn't get up for a while, though. I just lay there and glowered.

The place was trashed. Two trees wide might make an acceptable temporary shelter—better than I had the first month I was here—but damned if I wanted all that experimentation and work to go down the tubes. Ugly visions of a full week of finding a new site and preparing just a beginning lean-to filled my mind.

I cursed for about five minutes. Finally I got all the vinegar out of my system, got up, and started to untangle the tarp. There was only one rip in it, and it was along an edge. Tough stuff.

I searched out my belongings and piled them up. The batteries I put off to one side, and when I finished picking up everything else, I spent a little time experimenting with the tree stump. The power from one battery caused a slow but visible breakdown of the plastete. I walked over to a different plastete tree, a smaller one. No apparent result. I scratched my head, then went back to the rest of my stuff, got some wire, and hooked six power packs up in series. Bingo. It started pulverizing immediately and kept right on turning to powder. I jumped out of the way just in time.

However it is the stuff ages, a good zap of electrical current really speeds it up. I suppose there's a tiny little battery at the heart of each tree, regulating how soon it'll come down. Battery-operated trees. It wasn't in the literature, but it's cute.

I'll have to keep this in mind next time there's a lightning storm. I wonder if they thought of that when they were designing the things.

Once again I stretched the tarp into some semblance of shelter around the remaining two trees and the big front rock. I put the power packs back in my clearing, draped tarp over them, and went off in search of breakfast. The stuff I'd had ready to eat had been ground into the dirt.

"South America," she typed into the terminal. "Jungle." The computer narrowed down the possibilities of what she was looking for and gave her data. It was not much more than the fluff she had heard in the media: the death of the jungles around the world, the international effort to make an effort to save some remnant of them—although the oxygen problem had been solved—as a good-hearted gesture to the world that had birthed humanity. It was a good, knee-jerk issue, and did well on most people's computer voting profiles, as long as too much money wasn't spent on it.

It was a fake. But it cost relatively little to put together, once Brazil had consented to sacrifice the land.

Clones were taken from the small bunches of trees left in the few pockets of jungle remaining. Animals were donated from zoos. Artificial, biodegradable trees were adapted from existing technology to fill the gaps until the imported plant life grew to maturity. All this was put onto land fenced off and renewed at fair expense.

The computer assured her that it would be a good climax jungle in a matter of decades, albeit a mixed, homogenous one. It also assured her that everyone was satisfied with the effort.

People were not allowed in the Jungle. It was not controlled for human habitation, and human interference could nullify the pure scientific aspect which put the project a little higher on many voters' profiles.

"Brasilia, Brazil," she typed. "Airfare."

Bananas. Grubs. A big turtle which I decided to save for dinner. Then I took a muddy swim in the river, thought about my next home, dripped dry, dressed, went back to the clearing and discovered the man.

He had a weapon at his side, but he didn't look like he thought he'd need to use it. He was dressed in pressed jungle khaki.

I just looked at him. I didn't know what to do.

He was sweating and looked uncomfortable. "This isn't my job," he said. He sounded upset.

"Why don't you go do your job, then?"

"Public opinion is that you shouldn't be allowed to stay."

I walked carefully into the clearing, keeping an eye on him. He kept facing me, and he didn't take his hand from his weapon.

"Does everyone know I'm here, then?" The thought surprised me.

"No. But they've run projections. The longer you're here the less likely it is we can keep a lid on it. Public opinion will be bad when it comes out. So you've got to go."

Even killing robots made me feel guilty at first, since I knew they were just trying to disable me and take me out of the Jungle. I didn't think I could bring myself to kill this person—even if he'd had no gun. I moved slowly, so as not to make him panic, past him into the center of the clearing. His eyes darted away now and again, as an insect flew close or a plant rustled, but came back quickly to fix on me.

"How do you know what people will really think, if you don't let them make the decision?" I could throw a dagger at him, maybe even hit, although I've never had much luck with that. But if I didn't kill him or completely disable him, he was the one with the gun.

"Grow up," he said in an irritated voice. "Live in the world."

"I'm trying," I said. He wiped sweat from his jaw, a fastidious movement, and suddenly I could see what I looked like to him: mud-grayed skin, a wild tangle of partly tied-back hair, rags of a once-trendy shirt and pants. More muscled than I'd ever been. An animal.

"Will you come back without fighting?" he asked, using the tone reserved for small children and unstable people. "There's plenty of help waiting for you outside."

"All right," I said. "Let me get a few things."

She stood at the border of the Jungle. She could barely see anything past the fence in the dark.

She had to decide now. Was she a tourist taking a spicy, forbidden look at an off-limits site? Had she indulged in a fantasy when she bought camping odds-and-ends at the approved camping grounds and brought them with her? She could get past the electrified fence, but it would be painful.

Her legs ached. This was not a part of any route her rental car would drive her to. She'd abandoned it a dozen kilometers back, at the nearest point the computer would drive the car. It was probably already relaying the alarm at her absence.

She looked down at the key card that operated the car. Her name and picture were on it. She'd always hated the name Nikkie. There was a long ID number after the name.

She ripped it up and picked up her sack.

I smiled at him, picked up the tarp in the clearing, and went into the lean-to. He watched me go in.

I put the contents of the tarp against the left-hand tree, careful to position it just right. Then I picked up a couple of things, including my dinner, and went back outside.

"Can I just look around for a few moments?" He was about to respond when I yelled "Look out!" and the tree came crashing to our left. I was on the right. While he gaped at the huge plummeting tree, I brought my nice turtle dinner, still in the shell, square down on his skull.

He wasn't badly hurt, although the turtle was ruined. I bandaged his head with his shirt, then dragged him in a fireman's carry toward the nearest perimeter. I found a pen in his pocket, and I wrote on his forearm:

"Out is toward the banana bush and straight from there. So long. Don't call."

He was beginning to stir when I slipped off.

The gun should come in handy for protection while I'm building the next shelter. I've got some pretty good ideas for it. I suppose it's too much to ask that the next guy bring an axe. I sure could use one.

The Big Wish

Later it would be cold comfort that she had never tried to fall in love. Love was a complication. Marianne had been content to live alone.

Then came Geoffrey, and there was no doubt that he was wonderful and he loved her. She had lived with him for almost a year when she went to New York to take summer computer courses, for her tech writing; and there she met Vince. She never intended to fall in love with him, either.

Clearly there was a crisis. She told Geoffrey about Vince–they kept no secrets–and Vince knew about Geoffrey. Each waited in his different way for her decision.

Marianne waited until final exams were over, reserved a motel room in Queens. She stared at the graffiti in the subway car. She signed in, collected her key, found her room and closed the door behind her to think.

When Marianne was very young she knew a secret. All her friends knew it too; but as they used it and forgot, she remembered.

When Marianne was four years old a circus came to town. She and Crystabelle saw a commercial for the circus on a Saturday cartoon show.

"Wow," said Crystabelle.

They were figuring out the difference between cartoon people and real people that summer. Cartoon people lived somewhere flat where you could never touch them, but real people you could touch and talk to. The spangled acrobats and tumbling clowns in the commercial were really out there somewhere– "coming soon to the

Ampitheatre."

But Crystabelle's mother said the circus was out of the question this year, honey. So did Marianne's mother.

"I want to do it," Crystabelle said. "I want to see the elephant. I want to be in the parade!"

Marianne did too, but she held back. "Next year maybe," she said.

"*This* year," said Crystabelle. And she screwed up her face and made her wish.

The next week Marianne watched on television as really Crystabelle, not a cartoon, rode in the brightly-colored box on the back of the elephant. She was hurting with envy, but she remembered: that was Crystabelle's only wish.

When Crystabelle's family had to move to Kentucky five months later, Marianne gently reminded her that she wouldn't have had to move if she hadn't used up her wish. Crystabelle stared through her tears and said, "Don't be funny."

"You shouldn't have used your wish for the elephant."

"I rode the elephant because I won the coloring contest!" shouted Crystabelle. "Stop lying!" Marianne tried to make her remember, but Crystabelle hit her hard on the arm and ran off.

Marianne had spent the rest of the day tucked inside the little closet under the staircase, thinking.

Marianne and Geoffrey fell naturally into togetherness. Sex was warm if unspectacular, and they talked about everything. Geoffrey listened to her fears and dreams, and he made her feel more comfortable with both than she had ever been.

She even thought she might tell him about the secret—but she could never quite bring herself to talk about it. Wishing seemed silly when you were a grownup. And while she and Geoffrey were silly and childish and giggly, she didn't want to be silly and serious at the same time. He would have forgotten like everyone else.

Who first mentioned marriage? Probably neither of them. They both began planning for it without either proposing.

As everyone said, Marianne and Geoffrey were meant to be.

o o o

In kindergarten wishes began snapping like flashbulbs. Eddie Tannenbaum got a sharp red two-wheeler, but it took him a year to learn to ride it. Lisa McKay's family adopted not one but two puppies; the next week a litter of kittens was born on Elaine Marx's back porch, and she was allowed to keep them all. Both girls grew bored with the pets, and gave most of them away. Bill Coleman's parents reunited; Marianne, pursing her lips, allowed silently to herself that that was probably a good enough thing to spend your only wish on.

And in five wild weeks, Sandi, Arnold, Sharon and Meg each had birthday parties successively bigger and grander than the last: very exciting, and quickly passed.

The last of her classmates' wishes went for Tony Patterson's three-run homer in Peewee League. Tony was still talking about it two years later in fourth grade, by which time most of the kids avoided him. He hadn't hit a home run since.

Marianne watched the wishes dry up, and made notes. A wish was a one-time thing, so it had better be important. And there was no going back once you made it—no Oops, let me try that again. Which must be why people didn't want to remember that their wishes were gone. There would most always be something in the future more worth wishing for. None of the things wished for seemed important once the wish was used up.

She tended her wish, held it against the future, and promised herself that when she used it, it would be big. Really big.

The motel door closed behind Marianne and she began thinking of Vince. She felt she ought to be thinking of Geoffrey, too, but Vince filled her thoughts, the entire field of vision inside her head, and she could not remember what Geoffrey looked like. He was handsome, she remembered that much.

Vince was not handsome. Rugged, perhaps. Charismatic, certainly; he dominated a room, made everyone laugh. It was exciting to be with him; all eyes were always on them. But not physically her type at all: burly-chested, thick-waisted. His hands were wide and dark, olive tan; she could see his hand against the very pale skin of her upper arm, squeezing a little too tight, hurting a little. Marianne's breath quickened at the sudden clearness of the tactile and visual image. She hated it when he used too much strength, but she knew he didn't mean to; his moments of roughness made her tender toward his frequent gentleness. And her tenderness would burn deeper–

She didn't know what to do with this unaccustomed passion. Hormones, she told herself. Doctor, the problem is that I have a little bit of blood running through my hormone stream.

"It's a short quarter, but it's still five weeks," Geoffrey had said. "That's a long time. If anything happens–I'll understand." It was a short time and nothing could possibly happen, she had told him, lovingly, securely. And ten days later, in her daily phone call home, she was crying, telling him that a man she had just met had fallen in love with her. Geoffrey was the only person she could cry with. "But that's not the worst thing."

"What?" he asked, his voice very quiet.

"Maybe–me too."

He hadn't complained, hadn't shouted. He told her it was her choice; he wanted her to be happy. He did not weep, but she did. She could not imagine crying with Vince. Vince made her feel tough, feel New York, made her life with Geoffrey seem puzzlingly soft.

"What do you want from me?" she had asked Vince, his strong dark arms circling her from behind.

"Leave him. Marry me." He touched her engagement ring: "No. But I wish you could."

It hurt, and it was a stupid, stupid problem.

The solution was simple: Geoffrey had prior claim. She knew they would be happy together. She knew, despite his stoicism, he would be miserable if she left.

The solution was simple: obey her most urgent needs.

She threw a bed pillow hard across the room. It knocked over a table lamp.

The solution was inescapable.

"Will you always love me?" asked Geoffrey, Vince.

"Yes," she said.

о о о

She felt faintly ridiculous. She had never seen an adult make the wish. Children could approach wishes with wholehearted faith, but she had no idea how to go about it.

She turned off all the lights, turned on the heat lamp in the bathroom. A red glow bled from the half-open door. She stood before the mirror on the closet and stared at herself, a tall, narrow young woman, backlit in artificial sunset, her shoulder-length brown hair turned to copper. She opened her mouth.

"I wish–" She broke off. Did she really want to do this? She had saved this one chance her entire twenty-six years. It was her only wish.

Geoffrey, Vince.

"I wish I could be with both Geoffrey and Vince. Each. Equally. Completely. I wish."

Nothing happened. She closed her eyes and wished silently, hard. No. She opened her eyes. Suddenly she was afraid that she might have actually used it up when she was very small, and forgotten; or worse, that she had fooled herself with a childish dream all these years.

"Damn it," she whispered.

And it started. Vertigo almost toppled her; she grabbed the hall sinktop. Her head pounded.

She felt she was peeling away from herself; she felt like two plies of tissue being gently separated. In the mirror, her reflection wavered. She watched, confused, as it pulled slowly apart, becoming two Mariannes.

Each image of herself was slightly translucent. She looked away from the mirror and recoiled a step in shock at the sight of herself right in front of her nose. Herself stepped back too. Which was she, the right or the left? The vertigo hit again; she concentrated on being one Marianne (right; left!) and it settled.

She backed away slowly, saying nothing. She was afraid of hearing the other's voice. She sat on the edge of the bed. The other righted the desk lamp and turned it on. Marianne, on the bed, wondered why the light was so dim. She looked at the lamp and saw two: one lit, one on its side, dark. The other Marianne was looking at the prone lamp. She reached for it; her hand passed through it. She moved the standing lamp an inch to the side.

Marianne on the bed walked to the desk—carefully passing her twin, who pulled back against the wall—and stood the fallen lamp. It and the other were not quite aligned; looking at them made her feel her eyes were crossed, although the rest of the room was in sharp focus. The lighted lamp, transparent to her eyes, had no substance to her hand. The other was solid and real. She lit it and the room brightened. She returned to the bed and ripped off the bedspread. The bed stayed ghostily made. Other Marianne attempted to pick up the rumpled quilt and failed. She touched the one on the bed, slowly drew it back, replaced it. Her counterpart could see the white sheets through the patterned cloth.

It was not what she expected—but now she could have both lives. She could change her life. Vince. Heat spread from her stomach, to make her heart flutter, to make her groin clench. Vince.

They caught each other's eyes. She could see through her twin, but that Marianne was as real as she, lived in a world as urgent as hers, wanted what she wanted. One must go home to Geoffrey. A sense of loss surprised her; if she went off with Vince she would not see Geoffrey again. She thought of holding him, lips soft against his neck, his little purring sound.

Who would go where? She pulled a coin from her pocket. The other shook her head. To assign a man to a side meant one of them would have to break the silence. As she hesitated, the other took a pad of paper with the hotel imprint—a solid pad remained on the bedside table—and scribbled VINCE under the imprint, GEOFFREY on the plain white bottom. She ripped the paper horizontally, jumbled the pieces behind her back. Marianne pointed to one side. She mutely held out the scrap with the verdict. Marianne picked up her suitcases and went her separate ways.

Two Mariannes going to the man she loves. The relief on Geoffrey's face; the whoop of astonishment from Vince.

She holds him, holds him; she can't get enough of him, it seems. She does not think about the other man. She will not think about the other man. That belongs to another her.

Now and again he asks her what she is thinking, and she makes a joke and turns the subject away. She has always been good at diverting attention. She turns it away from her own mind, time and time again.

Marianne and the man she loves. Everyone remarks on how well-suited they are.

When Geoffrey met her at the airport she was unable to find him in the crowd. He kissed her and took her carry-on bag before she realized he had been standing right in front of her as she looked through the strange faces. His face was no less strange to her than any other.

She spent the next weeks in a daze. This quiet, gentle person— who was he? Why was she with him? Where was the passion of the month before, the dizzy excited high?

"Is something wrong, honey?" he asked.

Marianne turned quickly from the dresser mirror. "What? Oh. No."

"All right," Geoffrey said, taking off his socks, but he looked at her with concern in his eyes. She never could hide anything from him. She rarely wanted to.

"I'm sorry," she said. "My mind is—somewhere else."

"Oh," said Geoffrey. She was silent for a while, pulling the covers up to her chin. "You know," Geoffrey said quietly, "you could fly to New York. You could afford a few days off."

"The wonders of being self-employed," she said wryly. "I could, but I don't think it would be good business practice."

"Who's talking about business?"

"Wasn't that the topic?" she said, knowing he'd see through her light tone but trying anyway.

"You've hardly mentioned Vince at all since you came home." She stiffened. "Sorry. If you'd rather not—"

"It's okay," she said. "I just don't think I should impose it on you."

"It's what I'm here for," he said. He tossed his pants in the hamper and got into bed. He lay curled away from her. She reached out and flicked off the light. He said, "If you ever change your mind—"

"Oh, sweetie," she said. She put her arms around him, pulled him against her. "My beauty, my darling, it's okay, I chose you. . . ." She rocked him gently until he was asleep, and all she could see was the crumpled scrap of paper: GEOFFREY. "I chose you."

Twice she caught herself with her hand on the phone. When she realized who she was about to call, she dropped the handset into the cradle and started picking up the room, scraping old paint off the windowsill, anything busy. Working to breathe.

But it passed, each time it passed; she told herself it must pass entirely soon enough. She had chosen Geoffrey, one way or another, and with Geoffrey she would stay. When she was at home, alone, like now, and her work was finished, she had little else to do but repeat that to herself. And stay away from the phone.

The phone was in her hand. "Hello?"

"Hello," she said automatically, and she knew numbly that she had called Vince. There was a long, fuzzy pause on the line.

"Marianne? God, Mari, is that you?" His deep voice climbed half an octave with delight. She couldn't think what to say. She was having trouble breathing again. "It's been a month—five weeks—I didn't think I'd hear from you. It is you, isn't it?"

Of course. She remembered two slightly different motel rooms, one solid, one indistinct. Her Vince was still alone.

"Mari?"

Marianne hung up. Talking to this Vince would tell her nothing. She would have to see them, their images, in person. That was what she wanted to know, that was why she had called. She had to know. She had to find out what she had lost, coming out on the wrong side of her wish.

She had been blocking it out of her mind, like Crystabelle had so many years ago. But hadn't she wished better than Crystabelle?

Marianne packed just a few things, quickly before she could change her mind. She did leave a note: "Hon, you were right, I do need a vacation. Just a few days. If Lloyd calls, tell him he'll get the manual by the twenty-third. Don't worry about me. I'll try to call. Love you intensely, M."

In the cab to the airport she thought intense thoughts. Of Vince.

o o o

It was the same motel, but a different room. Because it was late, Marianne spent the night there. The next morning she went to the desk and asked for room forty-one. The clerk groused, but exchanged the keys.

The bed looked ordinary. She looked over at the lamp. There was something about it. She moved it. Its ghostly image remained.

Marianne sat straight down on the floor, hugging the solid lamp to her chest. She wasn't crazy. There was a world in which everything was as another Marianne had caused it to be, and here in the same city as the other Marianne, she could see it.

She was almost at Vince's building when the flaw in her plan struck her, too late. Vince emerged from a laundromat across the street. She ducked into a florist's and busied herself staring at the bright tiger lilies in the display case. A hand squeezed her shoulder.

"Hi. Shopping for me?" She stood still. "Excuse me. You are Marianne Bruner?" His hand pulled and she turned, slowly, and looked at him, not breathing.

He arched an eyebrow. "Hello, again. Fancy meeting you here."

"Hello, Vince." She was fascinated by the iron calm in her voice. His hand remained on her shoulder, feeling absurdly warm.

"Why didn't you tell me you were in town when you phoned?" The laundry gave off a damp, soapy smell. By a slight effort of concentration, she could smell either soap or roses and carnations. She could abstract his magnetic voice, look right into his eyes.

"I'm sorry I disturbed you." His eyes were green ringed with brown; with a little more concentration, she could make them look as alien, unreal as Geoffrey had looked when she first got home.

"We're a block away from my place, you know. I don't think you got here by accident."

"I'm meeting a client."

"In a flower shop?"

"I thought I'd send Geoffrey some flowers. It's a year since we met." Longer than that, but the lie came easily.

"A block from my apartment?"

"Near my client's office."

"Damn it, Mari!" He grabbed her other shoulder, gripped her

tightly. "You told me you had a decision to make, and then I never heard from you! Never! Now I find you hiding out in my neighborhood. You told me you were big on honesty—I'd like to hear some!"

How his temper angered her. She wanted to shout at him. She wanted to bury her head in his shoulder. She opened her mouth with no idea what she would say.

"Excuse me. May I help you with something?" Marianne turned to see a plump Oriental woman with a disapproving set to her lips.

Everything rushed back calm. "I'd like to wire a dozen red roses," she said smoothly. From the corner of her eye she saw Vince wrench his laundry to his shoulder and stalk out of the store. The shopkeeper watched him leave and smiled at Marianne.

"New York or out of state?"

"Out of state," she said, and mechanically finished the transaction.

She phoned Vince's apartment to make sure he was not there and let herself in with the copy of his key that she had kept.

Here, where the other Marianne must be living, she expected to see many ghosts like the lamp in the motel; but as she moved rapidly through the apartment, she found nothing. No ghost magazine where the other she had tossed it; no ghost tampons in the medicine chest. She moved rapidly from room to room, breathing with difficulty, not knowing whether it was from fear of Vince coming back, or from frustration and anger. Why was there no evidence of her twin here? Stupid, stupid! She would have gone straight to him. If the random chance had come out differently—Damn, damn, the wish was wasted.

A movement in the front room. She swallowed and hid behind the doorway, trying to think what to say to Vince when he found her. But there were no sounds, no footsteps. She peeked around.

Three transparent people walked around the kitchen. The shorter man had a dozen keys at his belt. They walked through Vince's furniture as they pointed and discussed the apartment.

Empty. There are no ghosts because the other apartment is empty, Marianne thought. We moved! Of course, we'd need a larger place.

She walked right through the woman on her way out.

o o o

It only took her a day to find them.

Vince did much of his writing for a large telecommunications company a short subway commute away. The first time she saw him arrive at the glass-walled office building, he was solid, her world's Vince. But an hour later another Vince walked up to the building, briefcase in hand. And another Marianne. The sun streamed through them.

Her heart pounded. She made herself wait, far down the block, until they finally emerged from the building; she followed them into the subway and sat well back from them in the car, where she had a three-quarters rear view of them, nervous that her counterpart would turn and see her.

But the other Marianne stared straight ahead with an expression Marianne recognized from feeling it on her own face: she was upset. She wanted Vince to notice. She needed him to ask what was wrong before she could tell him.

Vince did not ask. He sat with his own thoughts, unreadable to the spying Marianne.

They were living in the ground apartment of a two-flat. In real life it must still have been vacant, although it seemed someone had either moved a few of his possessions in or most of his possessions out: she saw a solid table, some chairs, a bureau, half a dozen cartons. The kitchen window, in her world, was not locked.

They were in the living room. Vince watched television, flipped through a magazine; she had papers on her lap, lining out sentences and writing new ones in. They didn't talk for a long time; finally she said something. He snapped an answer. She shook her head, violently. Marianne could just make out the faintest burr when she talked, nothing when he did. There was no way to tell what they were arguing about.

Marianne, concealed in a corner, pleaded silently with Vince. Whatever it is, if it's her fault, just tell her it's all right! Geoffrey would do it.

What Vince did Geoffrey would not: he threw down the magazine and grabbed her. She stared wildly at him. He kissed her and Marianne, behind the loveseat, watched her melt and felt herself melt as well. The passion had not faded. Oh lord, it had not. She closed her eyes and when she opened them the room was empty. Where? She found the bedroom and watched from the hall as he pulled off her sweater, pulled her jeans open, ran his rough hands over her body. She was moaning, Marianne could barely hear it; Marianne moaned too. He kissed her and entered her and Marianne felt more than ever the frustration, the terrible frustration, that she had not had him and never would, the tyranny of blind chance.

The woman on the bed cried out and Vince wrenched back and forward one last time and fell exhausted beside her. Marianne leaned against the door frame and let tears flow down her face. She wished she had not come to see this. She would never be able to give up her beautiful, thwarted memories of Vince.

When her vision cleared a little she focused on the phantom Marianne. She lay isolated on her side of the bed, pulled away from the sleeping man, clutching her pillow. Her face was slick with tears. She said something.

Marianne could just hear that single word.

"Geoffrey," she said.

Having Keith

She wants him, wants him; she knows she cannot have him and she wants him.

He always comes to the library on Tuesday afternoons, so Paula is there too. Sitting very straight in the carrel, she can just see him over the top of the partition. Look at the way his hair sweeps across his forehead in dark bangs; there, he turns to replace a book and she can see the curls move softly at the nape of his neck. Lord, he is beautiful. She remembers another glimpse of him, his sleek, tanned body. But that was not through her own eyes and she is not sure, just yet, that it was real.

He bends to pick another book from a low shelf, disappearing; she must hold herself down in her chair, not leap up; after all the holding back she must not make a fool of herself now. A breath, two breaths, three, and he reappears. Now she really breathes. Air in his absence gives no sustenance.

She will have him. It might be enough just to see him, breathe his air, feel his presence, but soon enough he is bound to find out how she feels, and he will block her out completely, deny her even that. So she will find another way. That glimpse of him as though through other eyes, something she has not experienced since she was three–

He does not want her. While she was falling unwillingly in love with him he was falling enthusiastically in love with another.

She will find another way.

That sudden vision of Keith had been such a shock she could not sustain it. It was just his back, disappearing through a bathroom door; but it was unmistakably him, his long soft hair damp and tousled, and Paula had gasped in her bed while he melted away and was replaced by the speckled drapes of her tiny apartment.

She closes her eyes and thinks of Patty. Light brown hair and smiling light brown eyes, exactly like Paula but forever three years old. Patty and Paula were so close that they never thought it was strange they could see through each other's eyes, and they were so young adults never took anything they said about it seriously. Only years later did Paula learn that most people couldn't do anything like that.

The last thing she saw through her twin sister's eyes was the powder blue Dodge careening around the corner, straight at her. Little Paula screamed and fainted; when she woke, she was a singleton.

It was a painful memory. But Patty was gone forever, and she had learned long ago that it was no use thinking about her.

The vision of Keith is still with her, an image burned into her brain. Droplets of water glisten on his tanned and leanly muscled back; he is just turning his head around, perhaps to say something. A towel is tucked around his waist. He has very good legs.

It has been seventeen years since she has seen anything through another person's eyes. She wonders if she could again.

"What are you doing tonight?"

Chicken-fried steak turns to bile in Paula's mouth. She gulps it down. Take a breath: one, two.

"Studying, Elaine," she says carefully, and makes herself look up.

Elaine: slender, petite, very blond, deep long-lashed grey eyes. Carries herself with confidence, assurance. As well she should.

She used to think of Elaine as her best friend.

"Great," says Elaine, blind Elaine, with sweet sincerity. "Do you want me to come over and work through calculus together?"

"No," she says. Two phonemes. "Thanks." Another five. Seven phonemes: see how good she is at talking to Elaine.

"Well, if your place is no good tonight you could come over to mine," says Elaine with the beautiful density Paula has come to loathe. "If it's before his night class, Keith will be there, but we can get a larger pizza." Enthusiasm warms her voice.

"No!" How can she lose control of two phonemes? A breath. "Thanks. I have to go to the library."

"Why?"

My god, stop talking, stop making me talk! "Research."

"What are you researching?"

"A paper."

"What class?"

Stop it! "Psych 204."

"Isn't that the paper you said you had to finish last week when I asked you to the movie?"

She has been keeping Elaine's heart-shaped face out of focus; even that becomes too much, and she turns to her steak, sawing her knife through straw-colored bread crumbs. "Professor Bell asked me to expand it." Twenty or thirty or god knows how many phonemes, too many, please jesus Elaine stop!

Elaine stops. Paula takes a bite, chews mechanically and swallows. Another bite. Silence. Against her will she looks up to see the other woman staring angrily at her.

"Fine, Paula. I'm sure I don't know what it is with you anymore. I won't bother you again." She stalks off, picture of self-righteous indignation. Why shouldn't she be? Paula is not going to tell her either.

Those were your eyes I saw through, weren't they, dear cruel friend.

Attacking the chicken-fried steak.

I can do it.

The day she met him is preserved as perfectly in her mind as a strip of film. She had noticed he was older than the rest of the class when he sat beside her in zoology; that was all the notice she intended to pay him. But something about him kept reminding her that he was at her elbow, and by the end of the class she decided to talk to him.

"Lunch?" How bold she felt!

"A meal consumed between breakfast and supper." He had a wonderful smile. "Are we getting pop quizzes already in this class?"

She laughed. "I know some places around here that beat the cafeteria. Are you interested?"

"Anything would. I like a woman who makes promises she can live up to."

She laughed again. "Elaine! Um—" She gestured.

"Keith."

"—Keith and I are going to hit Albert's. Want to come?"

Mistake! How she has replayed that sentence in her mind. If it is a film, it has white streaks and splice jumps and the soundtrack flutters.

"I should go to the bookstore—oh, heck, sure."

Elaine was safe. Although she and her boyfriend fought, everyone agreed they would never split up.

"Sounds fun," said Keith.

Over chilidogs at Albert's she discovered he was beautiful.

He had just returned to college to prepare for med school, an ambition he shared with both Paula and Elaine. "Twelve-year-old B.A.'s in history don't exactly get you into Johns Hopkins." He had been trapped in his father's business for a decade; now the excitement of his new life lit up his eyes. "I always swore I'd never be a paper-pusher, but when I got married it all just seemed to happen. Now that that's over—don't laugh!—I'm plunging right into good old '60's idealism: inner-city clinics, helping starving babies and pregnant kids and all that counter-counterrevolutionary stuff." He shrugged with self-deprecation, while his eyes crinkled all round. Paula felt more excited about med school than she had been since she was a freshman.

The tan and the weathering were from rock climbing. His hands were quick, dextrous: jazz piano. His hair, unfashionably long. She was amused, intrigued; this Keith person would make a wonderful new fantasy. Of course, she was busy with her own life, wary of complications; she couldn't afford to get caught up with another person busy with his.

So she laughed when Elaine brought up amusing anecdotes about her confirmed bachelorhood and the last few guys who had tried to change her mind. She shouldn't let this guy think she was *interested.*

(And the only person she had ever been that close to was Patty, and Patty had died.)

Somehow, would-be boyfriends led the conversation to his ex-wife.

"—finally she just left. Well, it made sense. When I wasn't working, I'd be climbing, or taking guitar lessons, or directing a community theater show—anything to keep from thinking about being trapped. She wasn't interested in any of those things. She wanted something else. After she left, I realized I did too." He blinked and looked surprised at what he was saying.

"Do you miss her?" Elaine asked softly.

"I don't know. It wasn't like I knew her anymore." Elaine's small pale hand covered his. "Yes." She squeezed; he sighed, shook his head, smiled at her.

That was when Paula realized she loved him; and, simultaneously, that it was too late.

Not too late. Not too late!

She opens her eyes to see her hands clenched in front of her on the scarred veneer of the carrel. (Her lie to Elaine became self-fulfilling and she is back in the library, an empty place without Keith.) She tries to think about anything else but it is no use. Whenever Keith invades her thoughts (which is most of the time), he comes flooding in everywhere at once. As, uninvited, does Elaine. "We're not actually *living* together," Elaine giggles in her mind, and at the same time Paula can see their apartments, his just down the hall—opening the door, seeing a closet full of clothes, a desk covered with papers—and no bed. No cot, no futon, not a goddamned sleeping bag. Why are they so damn coy?

No. —Keith chasing a frisbee (Elaine throwing it). Keith making a joke that breaks everyone at the table up (Elaine slapping his back). Keith staring somberly across the duck pond (Elaine sneaking up and making him smile).

No!

Channel the emotion. She breathes slowly and deeply, forcing herself to be calm. She counts, slowly, slowly; her breathing evens; she rests her head on her arms. Things begin to fade away, as she concentrates. Keith. *Her.* (And a distant echo of Patty.) She feels oddly buoyant as she drifts off. . . .

. . . .He smiles at her. He reaches out and strokes her face. She wants to laugh, or cry, or learn to dance like in the movies so she can dance like that.

A voice in the back of her head says, This is impossible.

Shut up.

He's blind to everyone but Elaine.

Go away!

It's not real.

I've *made* it real! and she grabs him and kisses him in a wonderful moist mess and when she pulls back finally her hair has fallen into a blond web over her eyes and she remembers how.

"Sweet Elaine," he says softly.

Not you, the voice says, and his beautiful face begins to fade.

Shut up, she thinks grimly. I'll make it me.

Blackness.

Despite a blinding headache she makes it home from the library. She should be elated at the first success, but the memory of the kiss is staggering, almost more painful than pleasurable, as when she was twelve and first considered that it was actually possible to kiss someone, thinking of a boyishly charming television star. The first visceral imagination of what that would be like had literally knocked her breath away, frightening her.

Even Keith's touch on her cheek eclipses that memory.

Not *your* cheek, says the nagging voice.

In any case, she must find out if it was genuine, not some trance-induced dream. She forces herself to seek out Elaine's company the next afternoon in the cafeteria. Elaine has forgotten or forgiven Paula's rudeness of the day before; Paula endures a stream of one-sided conversation—a conversation in which she is determinedly silent.

"—funny thing is that he thinks he knows me so well, but he really doesn't."

If you loved him you wouldn't hide anything from him. I wouldn't.

"It's this whole love-at-first-sight thing. He did the same thing with his ex, you know. He didn't see that she wasn't what he thought until she left him, and he thinks I'm exactly the same image that came to him in one piece. Lucky it's a good one!"

I never fall in love at first sight. I always used to be safe from that.

"Anyway, I really think this will work out. I'll have to be careful, of course. His illusions are so precious to him. But he's got to stop that idiotic climbing. And this notion of staying friends with his ex is impossible, don't you agree? And the idea of starving with his patients in the ghetto! A lovely dream, but it makes a lot more sense if we take over my uncle's practice together. He'd get stubborn if I told him outright, but I'll get him to see reason."

Keep your fucking hands off him, you ungrateful scum! Paula bites the insides of her cheeks to keep her mouth shut and almost misses what Elaine is saying:

"Things I just couldn't tell him. Like—he thinks I'm so level-headed—but last night I just flaked out. We were studying and I *swear* I didn't have anything in mind but all of a sudden all my clothes were off! He said he never saw me so aggressive. I don't even remember starting it! Just a blank. Scary. It's finals stress, I guess. You won't tell, will you?"

Paula stares at her. "This was last night?" Elaine nods. "About what time?"

"I don't know—nine or so—why?"

Bingo! "If it only happened once I wouldn't worry about it."

"You're probably right." Elaine looks relieved. "It's so nice to have someone I can tell something like that to."

You should trust him with things like that. You don't deserve him. The thought comes with a rush of warmth, a rightness. She thinks it again, clearly. You don't deserve him.

I deserve him.

She pushes her bedtime forward, spends each night meditating, trying to project herself onto Elaine again. The results are mixed: a glimpse of his face one, twice; Elaine's small hands washing in the sink; class notes; an oddly-angled view of his foot. No contact as sustained as the first, and in the mornings she is very tired, as though she had not slept. Still, she takes strength from the small successes.

One night she finds herself sitting on the edge of the sofabed. The scene is hazy, the contact unstable. She looks up and Keith is at the door. It starts to slip away. Quickly she jumps up, slams the door in his face, double-latches and chains it before she loses touch.

Awakening, exhausted, she can still see the astonishment on his face.

That morning Elaine is very pale.

Keith approaches her after zoology and everything clenches inside her. She has not spoken to him in class since, inevitably, he chose Elaine as his lab partner. "Has Elaine talked to you today?"

"No. Why?" Her hand remembers the feel of his neck, his hair.

"Nothing. She just was—a little strange, last night. It's not important." He smiles innocently at her; it hurts; at the same time she feels triumph. She is no longer powerless. The knowledge gives her confidence. She smiles back at him.

"Do you want to go out to lunch?"

"Well," he says, looking back where Elaine is cleaning up their table, "I'm not sure she's up for it now. I can ask her."

It is the longest conversation she has had alone with him. Every nerve is stretched, humming. "Do *you* want to go to lunch. I didn't ask her."

He frowns a little. "I can hardly leave her alone right now."

"It might be a good idea. Anyone who slams a door on you with no explanation—"

"I thought she hadn't talked to you."

That's right. She is so fatigued; she forgot. She rushes over the lapse. "Maybe you should spend time with other people. You've spent so much with her, you can't know what other people might have to offer."

He is really looking at her now, straight at her. It dizzies her, looking at his eyes. "What are you saying?" he asks quietly.

Why not, she asks herself. What is there to lose, anyway? She opens her mouth, cannot speak.

"You?"

"Yes," she says in a tiny, odd voice. "If you could only look past her for once—if you just saw what I could—"

"I see." His voice is distant.

"I mean, look at her! Having blackouts, acting irrationally, trying to cover it up—"

"You'd really use this against her."

"You don't know her! She wants to change you, she wants to destroy you—"

"If Elaine needs help, I'm going to see that she gets it. And the first thing to do is protect her from her supposed friends. I think," he says, his eyes chilly, opaque, "it would be best if you don't see her anymore." He turns his back on her. He collects Elaine, who follows with uncharacteristic passivity, and walks out of the classroom without another word.

I don't want to see her, I want to see you! Oh lord, I blew it, I finally ruined it all. She slides down against the blackboard and cries silently in the empty classroom.

Again she walks home alone, always alone. There is thunder and then rain pours down on her. She seeks no shelter; let the storm crash against her. She passes their building and sees a light in Elaine's apartment. She stops to stare at it for a while, thinking irrelevantly that no one could know there are tears among the rainwater streaming down her face: although she has destroyed her own façade, the storm has kindly given it back to her. The wind plasters her shirt and jeans to her chilled skin. She stares until the pain tops over and runs out of her like rainwater, and walks on. Near her own building a bare-chested young man is washing his hair in the squall; he flicks suds at her and his friends laugh. "Hey, lady," they call. "Hey, lady!" She keeps walking, their laughter following her.

Her apartment repels her with its emptiness. All or nothing, she thinks. She opens the oven door and blows out the pilot light; she lifts the stove top and extinguishes that one too. She turns all the dials. She is quite calm, because she knows what will happen: she will fail to keep contact with Elaine, return to her own body and open the windows; or she will stay until there is no body to return to. She has raised the stakes so there can be no failure. It makes perfect sense.

The smell is appalling but she ignores it, closes her eyes, breathes slowly. Keith. If he can only see good in Elaine who is bad for him, only feel disdain for her love, she will be Elaine. The blackness behind her eyelids deepens.

o o o

Black forever.

It would be easy, but she does not forget to concentrate. This is not like anything she has ever attempted before.

Black.

There is an arm. It does not want to move: she makes it move. There is a leg. Slowly, grimly, she straightens it. There is Elaine. She refuses it. She will not allow it. Fear, pleading, a horrible tearing and it is—yes! Gone! —And there is pain, and vertigo, and redness, and black again.

The bed feels wrong. Everything feels wrong, as though she is starting a bad cold. Worse.

Finally she opens her eyes. At first she thinks there is something wrong with her vision too: the ceiling is too close, the wrong shade. She swings her legs to the floor and almost falls: her balance is skewed. She grips the headboard—sofa back—and pulls herself to her feet. It has finally gotten through her brain, which seems as sluggish as her body, that she has made it. This time she is here for good.

She takes a breath—it feels odd, insubstantial in Elaine's narrow, confining ribcage—and goes to the bathroom, leaning a hand on the wall to keep from falling. Her coordination is that of a two-year-old. Elaine's face stares unreadably at her from the mirror. Her stomach lurches. *Elaine's* stomach lurches: the thought rises like bile.

The face is pasty, almost bloated; the grey eyes inhumanly pale; how can Keith find this attractive? She finds the makeup, yanks out the drawer, overcompensating for the weaker body, spilling trays and tubes of makeup. She gathers them clumsily in shaking hands.

She opens all the makeup and applies it furiously, trying to soften the big yellowish eyes with eyeshadow, smearing on blusher to narrow the cheeks—to look like Paula. She stares at the results: a dimestore china doll, sloppy, lifeless.

There is a knock on the door. Her heart (Elaine's heart, flabby in her chest) jumps. She calls out: "Just a second!" The voice is high-pitched in her ears. She cannot tell if it sounds natural.

A pause. "Are you okay?" asks Keith's voice.

She swallows. "Yes. I'll be right out."

She takes off the nightgown. The breasts are small but too heavy, too low. The waist is too narrow and the thighs are heavy and the ankles are *puffy*. Where is the little scar above the navel (never such a deep and puckered hole)? The pallid skin smothers her. The room darkens and she realizes she is hyperventilating; she grabs for the toilet tank with short white arms. The icy porcelain is friendlier than Elaine's clammy, alien flesh.

Keith's voice is calling a name that is not here. A key scrapes in the lock.

"Elaine? Honey?" Muscular arms circle the narrow naked waist and she shudders, squeezes the eyes tight. She feels how small the mouth is as it tightens into a rictus, and shakes harder. She is turned around. "What have you done to your face?" His hand strokes the cheek. In all her fantasies his hand on her face felt like his hand on *her* face. He half-carries her to the sofa, a warm, firm forearm supporting the heavy breasts. He squeezes and she feels Elaine's nipples respond, harden, with a life of their own. She jerks away, lurching to her feet.

"Elaine?" Through Elaine's eyes he is distorted, Picasso by way of El Greco. He reaches for her but she evades him somehow and is in the bathroom, throwing the bolt.

But in the bathroom is the mirror, the monster staring at her. The banging on the door, the shouts of an alien name, sound very far away. A can of shaving cream sits on the sinktop, and not having to think about it she grabs it, smashes it into the mirror.

"Elaine!"

One long shard of glass nestles in the spreading foam. She picks it up slowly. She thinks of Patty, whom she will finally join. And she thinks: Keith, you beautiful idiot. There is a faint smell of gas.

She wakes up. Wakes up? Then she has had the worst nightmare of her life, and is cured forever of a sordid fantasy.

Her limbs feel long again, too long after the impossible confinement of that little body—her own body feels foreign after the ordeal. She waits for normalcy.

But who is she holding? Who is so cold?

She opens her eyes, and is met by Elaine's smiling empty stare.

Her arms around Elaine are tanned and muscular; dark bangs

sweep across her vision.
    And so she is successful.
    She has Keith.

Over The Long Haul

Sometimes I think I've been in this truck forever, but of course that's not so. I just have to look at my license card if I want the proof: "Shawana Mooney," it says, and right next to that the day I got the card, two years ago. Two weeks after little Cilehe was born, which makes it easy to remember her birthday.

That name "Shawana" makes me think sometimes my daddy was a guy named Shawn Parker. My mama sure cried when he got shot dead when I was eight, but she wouldn't say he was my daddy. She just said he was no good and ran drugs and then she cried some more. Mooney, of course, that's my mama's name and her mama's, and it was my great-grandma's too. Also my great-grandpa's. They were married. Then the card's got my picture, which looks terrible with my eyes all starey the way the camera caught them, but I kind of like the way I had my hair done then, with all those little braids my grandma put in.

I must look awful now. I look at myself in the big side mirror when I fix up my makeup, but I don't really look hard at the whole effect, if you know what I mean. When Tomi gets a little bigger—he's barely four now—maybe I can teach him to fix my hair.

Or maybe we'll get out of this truck.

I think about that a lot, especially when Cilehe gets cranky and yells. Which isn't fair to her of course because what two-year-old wants to grow up in the cab of a truck, six feet wide and six feet deep? Sure, she's got Sesame Street like I did—and a lot of other much more boring TV, like it or not—but I could go outside besides, even if my grandma was always warning me about gangs. Cilehe's the kind of baby who needs to move around and tire herself out, which is pretty hard here.

I know exactly how she feels.

But it's none of her doing. I tell myself that. I got her by my own self—well, I had help, but it isn't her fault her daddy isn't in a truck too. They put the welfare parents who actually are raising the kids in the trucks. Now, do you know any guy who's going to take them? Nope. Both their daddies were long gone before that happened.

One truck stop looks a lot like another. I was kind of dozing behind the wheel when it took a big pull right and the truck went off to an exit. I tried to guess where we were—I thought maybe Nebraska. Sure was flat as hell out there.

Cilehe started kicking up a fit. She always acts like the last couple minutes before we stop is a couple of hours, and screaming will make the truck go faster. The only thing that could make the truck go faster is if I hit Manual Override and drove it myself, and I'd better have a damn good reason for that or it's big trouble. She was screaming for the potty. She just started with that, and she doesn't like the portapotty in the cab. Me neither. I don't care what they say, the thing smells.

Got her in before she messed up her panties, Tomi following quiet as a mouse. He's not quite big enough to send into the boy's room alone yet. Then she didn't want to wash her hands, and when I made her she got her hands and face and hair and t-shirt and the floor all wet, and glared up at me like I did it. She stomped out of the bathroom with her sneakers going squish, squish, squish.

I looked in to see if I knew any of the drivers. Kimberlea and Avis were both there, still going along the same route I was. I met Avis for the first time in Minneapolis on this run. Kimberlea I met soon after I started. The women on the road tell me you can go forever between seeing someone twice, so that was lucky. As long as we kept going along the same route, taking our full breaks—who wouldn't take her full break?—so they'd be the same length, we'd keep meeting up. Kimberlea is older than my mama, maybe forty, and she used to do data entry in the very last office that still used it, years and years after everyone else stopped, until the business was sold and they retired the old-time system. Her kids are twelve and eight, and she was even married when she had them.

Avis was having trouble with her boy. Her one-year-old twins were in the big playpen in the middle of the dining room, the boy screaming his head off. I looked at Cilehe, but she just stared at the kid with big round eyes, didn't copy him. The baby wailed, while Avis drank Coke with her face turned away from him, her eyebrows down and her mouth real tight, trying to act like the baby wasn't there.

"But I don't know if I want green or blue," she was saying to Kimberlea.

Kimberlea sighed. "Girl, what do you need with neon fingernails?" I put Cilehe in the pen, away from Avis's boy, and let Tomi sit next to me.

"Just because I'm stuck in a truck all day doesn't mean I can't look good!" Avis is a couple years younger than me, maybe seventeen.

"That sort of thing costs money. You don't get that much to save."

"So what else do I have to spend it on?"

"You can save it," Kimberlea said stubbornly.

"Right, and maybe in twelve years when my babies are teenagers and they let me out, I'll have a couple hundred bucks!" Avis took a long drink of her Coke. Kimberlea and I said hi. "So why not order the implant kit and have something now?"

"Couple hundred dollars is better than nothing. And you could save more than that."

"On what the government gives us?" Avis snorted and peeled open a Snickers.

"I save six dollars a week," Kimberlea said.

"You told us," Avis said.

Last stop, Kimberlea'd laid out her whole plans over breakfast. She's studying for her accounting license. Accounting's just a matter of using spreadsheets and stuff, she said, but they still make you study for it. The coursework costs, and then you have to get a license, which is a lot of money even before the bribes. She saves every penny. Doesn't even use up her food vouchers; sells the leftovers back to the government for half value, or sometimes to other truckers for two-thirds. Her plate had scraps of meatloaf and carrots. Not even Jello for desert. She stays husky just the same.

"What the fuck you want an accounting license for anyway?" Avis asked. "It's just minimum wage. Your oldest is thirteen next year, so you get out one way or another." Trucking's also a labor option for mothers with just one preteenager, but I've only seen a couple women who chose it when they didn't have to. They'd put her on some other workfare labor. Maybe sidewalk cleaning. That's what I did, five hours a day, before Cilehe. I used to hate it, but it's better than trucking.

Kimberlea took her paper napkin off her lap, folded it neatly and laid it on her tray. "I don't like being on welfare if I can work," she said. "Not this workfare joke, a real job. I always worked, until they took my job away. That's the way I know."

The boy was screaming so loud now even Avis couldn't ignore it any longer. "Shit," she said. She stuffed the rest of the Snickers into her mouth and went to get him.

Kimberlea and I talked for a couple minutes until her watch started beeping. "Back to the road," she said. She gathered up her two kids, who had been reading quietly at another table—don't know how she saves six bucks a week, if she buys them books—and left.

Avis came back. "Damn kid needed a new diaper," she said. "Where's old Kim Burly?"

"Her break was up."

"Stuck-up bitch." She wiggled her fingers in my face. "So do you think green or blue?"

Tomi tugged my arm and pointed. I was set to ignore him, but the room had gone quiet. I looked up.

There was a man in the dining room.

Maybe if you don't truck you don't know how strange that was. When I was little, I guess most truckers were guys. Then they came up with the remote-driving system, one guy in his living room controlling a dozen trucks. The unions kicked a fuss about that, of course, so everyone yelled at each other until they came up with a couple solutions: early retirement with heaps of compensation for the old truckers—lot of younger guys took that and went into other work—and retraining the truckers that passed the tests to be controllers at a big fat salary. At the same time, they passed a law that there had to be a driver in each truck. For manual override in emergencies, like that was going to happen. But nobody trusts computers and leastways unions.

Then came the Welfare Labor Act, the workfare act.

Bound to happen they put us in the trucks. It's boring. It doesn't pay shit–the controllers get the real money. We all know why they put us with two kids in the trucks. It's like, you get yourself one kid, they put you cleaning sidewalks or something and thinking on what happens if you get another one. You get another one anyway, and bam! into a truck. So now you're on the road all the time, only get out at a truck stop and see other drivers and they're all women too. A third kid is too many to live in a truck cab, so you'd get out, but how're you going to get a third one? Locking you in a convent couldn't work any better.

What they say is truck cabs are perfect classrooms, educational TV the kids (and their moms) can't get away from. Getting away from bad influences. Breaking the cycle of poverty.

What it's about is punishing us, keeping us away from that nasty stuff that got us here. We all know it. These are the same people who got abortion made illegal, and whittled down sex ed next to nothing. (Though from what my mama told me once before she moved on, people hardly used birth control even when they had teachers telling them about it.) They're punishing us, all right.

The proof is they didn't use to have the trucker's areas in the truck stops walled away from the parts for regular motorists. But after guys started hanging out, because we were free or sometimes even paid them, that changed. Now with the segregation and trucks never stopping except at stops and checkpoints, we never see guys that way. All before my time, anyway.

I never saw a guy trucking. As far as I ever knew, they didn't even *let* guys choose trucking.

Avis was staring. "Jesus, it's a man!" she whispered.

"Real good," I said. "You remember what they look like."

Maybe I hadn't, though. Oh, he was tall and he was fine. White, like Cilehe's daddy, but dark tan skin. Maybe Latin. His hair came down in a braid over one shoulder, thick and brown and shiny. Cheekbones cut high like a TV Indian's. He had tight old jeans on. The way they hugged his hips close you could imagine doing yourself.

Man, it had been too long since I'd seen a guy.

He walked over to an empty table across the room and a dozen pairs of eyes followed him. Nobody said a word.

One skinny girl with a baby on her hip went over and stared

down at him. "Truckers only in this room," she said in a mean voice.

That broke the silence. Everyone started up with catcalls, hisses and "Who *cares?*" The girl glared back at all of us. Some of them, when they get put in the trucks, actually buy the crap about our Evil Ways and get worse than any taxpayer.

The guy just smiled up at her so nice your toes curled. "You're right," he said. His voice was like caramel candy. He pulled out his trucker's card.

The girl's lips went white. She grabbed the kid up in her arm, pulled another off her chair and left the room.

"That is mine," Avis said, to me or maybe just to the universe.

"What are you talking about?" Her eyes looked like a cat's fixing to go after a mouse. Squintier than a cat's, though, in her pasty pimply face. No way a man so fine-looking would go for her.

Not that I was after him.

"Seventeen months," Avis said. No need to ask seventeen months since what.

I fluffed my hair up around my forehead. I knew it looked like hell.

Avis was already moving, plowing through a crowd of women all trying to look like they had some casual reason for happening to go over by that particular table at that particular time. It sure wasn't worth it to join the mob.

"Look after your sister," I told Tomi. I put him in the pen with the other kids. "I'll be back in five minutes. Need some fresh air."

"Me too, Mama?" he asked, but he's a good kid. He didn't complain. I didn't want fresh air, I wanted to get out of the room so my eyes wouldn't be all over that guy. Something got you in this fix, I told myself. You think you'd learn someday.

Even the place outside for truckers to walk around is separate from the place car drivers go to let their poodles piddle. Same sky, though, high and gray, the wind whipping around pretty good. I took a deep breath of windy air. I told myself I wasn't a kid anymore, fourteen and stupid like when Tomi's daddy got him on me. When that didn't work, I tried telling myself he had a whole truck stop full of girls to pick from. When that didn't work, I looked at my watch and told myself I only had another ten minutes in my break, and odds were this guy wasn't going the same way anyway.

I talked to myself until I had me just about convinced.

"Nice day," he said.

I didn't jump. I was great. "Sure, if you hate sun and like smog."

"Somebody must," he said, "or you wouldn't be outside in it."

I turned then. "Oh, I just get tired of girl talk all the time," I said.

"I wouldn't know," he said. The wind was strong enough to flop his braid around. Some of his hair was loose and blowing over his forehead. His eyes were the clearest lightest brown I'd ever seen. "The women always seem to stop talking when I come in."

"Yeah, well, they're easily impressed." I couldn't understand why he was out here with me. Couldn't understand why I was saying bitchy things to him, either.

"But not you, I guess," he said.

"I been around some."

"I can tell you're a woman of experience."

Was he laughing at me? He didn't look like it. I grunted in a worldly sort of way.

"Cal," he said, sticking his hand out. After a moment I realized it was his name.

"Shawana," I said. Took his hand. Right when I did I knew I never should have. Something about man flesh just feels different, and the skin of my hand, I realized, had been starved for the taste of it.

The rest of my skin started up a clamor.

He was still holding on to my hand, so I pulled it back. I tried to think of something regular to say. "Don't see a lot of guys trucking," I said. Oh, smooth. Real smooth.

"Well, you've seen me," he said.

"Don't you have to have kids to get a trucking license?"

"Yes."

I couldn't think of anything to say to that—or too many things: You got kids? How come you have them and not their mamas? Where are they—the mamas and especially the kids? What are you doing out here?

Maybe he read my mind a little. "The baby's in his crib in the truck. I didn't want to wake him."

"Just one baby?"

Cal nodded—the braid went swish, swish.

"How come you're trucking?" Maybe it was rude to ask, but I could have said it Why isn't his mama stuck with him like the usual course of events?, which would've been ruder.

He looked away, which showed off his sharp cheekbones against the gray sky just about perfect. "I needed time to be alone. To think."

"Well, you sure got that," I said. I couldn't not ask any longer. "I didn't think they let guys truck. I thought it was a mother's job."

He rubbed his face in his hands and the air seemed to get even darker. "She—Jess's mother died. When he was born."

Oh, shit. "Jesus, I'm sorry, I didn't mean—"

He looked back at me and tried to smile. "That's okay. You couldn't know."

"I'm sorry."

"Yeah. Well, that's the one exception to the guideline that unwed welfare mothers get all the trucks. If the mother's dead, they let the father do it." His mouth quirked with no smile to it. "After all, their big argument is that the truck's the ideal classroom, so they can't say no. It's for the good of the kid, right?"

I felt bad about my nosiness. The silence stretched out.

"Um, you miss her?"

"Well, it's getting better. I don't think she was going to marry me anyway."

"You were *engaged*?"

He shook his head. "But I thought I could get her to marry me after—" He stopped and looked straight up at the sky, blinking hard.

I grabbed his hand, saying some nonsense like I do when Tomi's crying. Here I'd just been thinking about this guy as a hot body. Then I was holding him and still saying soothing nonsense things.

My watch beeped. He pulled back.

"I gotta be going."

"I'm sorry. Usually I want to be alone, but sometimes it's hard— and in the truck stops there's always such a crowd—"

"It's okay," I said. "I hope things are better."

"Which way are you going?" he asked suddenly.

"How do I know? It's been west on 80, if that's any help. I think I may be going to Salt Lake. I've done that route once or twice."

"Maybe we'll see each other again along the route."

My face got warm. "There's no way to know that."

He smiled an I-know-things-you-don't smile. "I have ways of being more certain."

The watch beeped again. "Well—bye, Cal."

"Until we meet again," he said.

Cilehe was in a real bad mood from being left alone. Tomi was trying to make her laugh, meowing like a cat and rubbing against her feet. Don't know where he ever saw a cat. Maybe on Sesame Street. My watch was beeping steady now: if I didn't get into the truck in a big hurry I'd lose all my discretionary money for a week. I helped Tomi out of the pen, yanked Cilehe up by the armpit, and ran to the parking lot.

Cal was leaning against a big black truck like I'd never seen. He looked at us as we scrambled up into the cab. I pushed the button to say we were ready to go. The truck lurched and squealed out of the lot and onto the highway.

It was fractions on the TV—one half, one third, one quarter—over and over and over and over again. Tomi watched for a while. Cilehe just scowled and rocked back and forth. Usually I pick her up when she gets like that. But as long as she wasn't making noise, I had other things to think on.

Out in the walking area, holding Cal, I was just trying to make him feel better. Now it was over, I was noticing all the ways he felt to me. His thick braid of hair squeezed between our chests. His soft flannel shirt and the hard muscles underneath it. The man smell. The little raspy sound when his tight jeans rubbed on mine—

Another twenty minutes and there's no telling what might have happened.

But the road wore on and the fluttery feeling began to die away. The guy had acted like he had reason to think we'd be at the same truck stop down the road, but that was about as likely as running into a whole different guy would be. If only I'd run into him earlier—nearer the beginning of the hour lunch break. Next break would only be twenty minutes, to gas up the truck and grab a quick bite, and he was running more than twenty minutes behind me on the road even if he did go the same direction and stop at the same stop.

Unless he decided to cut his lunch short and get right back on the road—

I began to have another thought I maybe wasn't proud of, a

thought about getting us out of the truck.

We stayed on 80 like I'd guessed, which means the long way across Nebraska, not the best scenery for distracting the brain. Corn, wheat—it all just looks green at a distance. About twenty thousand fractions later, the truck pulled itself off.

I looked for the strange black truck, but of course it wasn't there. I'd've seen him pass me on the road. I gassed up, parked and took the kids into the stop.

Kimberlea wasn't there. Avis was. Didn't really know anyone else, so I sat next to her again.

"That guy left early," she complained.

"Maybe he had to go check on his kid," I said.

"How do you know he has a kid?"

"He's gotta have one or he wouldn't be trucking," I said. "If he didn't bring it in, it must've been in its crib."

"Not much of a parent, if he leaves his kid alone in his truck," Avis said.

I hadn't even thought about that.

"It was probably sleeping and he didn't want to wake it," I said.

"Why you want to defend him?" she asked.

I shrugged. "No reason. Just seemed to make sense."

"I don't care if he's a lousy parent or Nelly Nurture," she said. Nelly Nurture is the teenage star of a show on public TV who tells you how to eat when you're pregnant and how to take care of your babies. "I just care if his parts are all in working order."

Then who should walk in but Cal himself, which Avis saw before I did. "And it looks like a great time to find out!" She jumped up. I couldn't stand to look at the way she embarrassed herself. I wondered at him being right when he said we'd meet again down the road.

"Is this seat taken?" He'd come over to the table, Avis hovering behind him looking mad. More girls were beginning to gather.

"I don't think so."

He sat. "What do you know about teething pain?"

"Well, if you rub his gums it helps. And they sell this stuff in little tubes that numbs them up."

"Could you show me?"

So I took him over to the counter and showed him. He pulled out some vouchers to pay for it. I noticed he had a fat wad of them.

"Will you show me how to use it?"

I told Tomi to look after his baby sister again, and Cal and I went out to the lot, all those female eyes at our backs. There was his truck, black and somehow heavy-looking, without the regular Mack or Peterbilt symbols on it.

"Let's stop at your truck first—I have something I'd like to do."

I unlocked it. He opened the door and got in, reaching down his hand to help me up. Cool, firm hand.

First thing he did was fold down the playpen's walls. The pen is big enough to sleep two big kids, and my mattress behind it is big enough to sleep one fat woman. (I'm not fat.) Fold down the walls, and most of the cab is mattress.

"What are you doing?" I asked, though I thought I knew.

"You'll see," he said. On the right wall of the cab, where it had been covered up by the playpen's wall, there was a little panel. You almost couldn't see it even looking straight at it. The place he pushed to make it pop open didn't look any different from the rest of the wall. Inside was a number display, what they call liquid crystal, and a whole lot of tiny little switches. He started messing with them.

"What are you doing?" I asked again.

"Just a second." He messed around some more, closed up the panel and smiled at me. "Now your central controller's computer thinks you're still on the road and haven't even gotten here yet. Then it'll register you coming here and starting your break in forty minutes. You've got an hour before you have to get going again."

"How can you do that?"

"I've got a few skills."

"If you can do that kind of thing, why are you driving a truck? You could be making real money."

There was a glitter in Cal's eye. He bowed his head down low and said some woman's name—Ellen or something, it was hard to hear. I went over and held his head up against my chest, with his braid snaked over the crook of my arm. Murmured nonsense again. His arms came up around my back and my hands went down behind his jeans.

We used every last inch of that mattress space.

"Oh christ," I said later, "my babies have been in the stop all this time."

"They'll be okay," he said.

I put the rubber band back on his braid. I'd been playing with it. "They're never alone this long. And what about Jess?" He looked at me. "You said he had teething pain."

"Oh–my god, you're right. I'd better get to him." He started pulling his pants on.

"Do you want me to help show you how to use the medicine?"

"No, that's okay. I'm sure I can figure it out."

"It's no trouble–"

"The instructions are on the tube, right? You go get your kids." He looked at his watch. "You've got ten more minutes."

Ten minutes left! I hadn't been stopped this long in two years.

I left him off at his truck and he kissed me right out in public. "See you next stop," he said.

I hadn't even thought of seeing him again. On the trucking routes, he could have any action he wanted. But if I was his first since Ellen or Helen or whoever, maybe it actually meant something to him.

I felt a little bad about that.

Tomi was sitting in the big pen, holding Cilehe and crying. Not screaming or anything–his face was wet and he was hiccuping. When I came in I could see him trying to look brave. He also looked sur-prised–like he thought I was dead and was amazed to see me.

"C'mon, guys," I said. When we got out the big black truck was gone.

I had to raise the playpen walls, which took a while since I'd never had them down before. Finally I found the catch that did it. My watch beeped, I pressed the button and we started off.

Nebraska's a wide state. We probably had another whole stretch of it. At some point I noticed my watch had changed time an hour earlier –Mountain Time Zone. That's one way to measure progress: time travel. Another is to measure the money you save, but unless you're Kimberlea that's pointless. Just as pointless to measure by the calen-dar, since Friday's just like Wednesday's just like Sunday, and night is like day but dark and not as many stops.

Another is to measure the seasons go by. But you spend some time driving in the south where it's warmer in winter than North

Dakota is some summers. And you spend so little time outside that the weather might as well be television, except for rainstorms crashing against the cab's roof. The babies never get used to that.

Or you can measure the seasons of your own body. Now that means something, because I've always been as regular as clockwork.

For example, I knew it was just about twelve days before my next period.

The kids were fussy. Even Tomi. He wanted me to hold him and he wouldn't let me let go. Cilehe screamed. After an hour I blew up.

"If you don't shut up I'll drive off without you next time!"

Cilehe screamed louder. Tomi's eyes went round and he bit his lips in like he was afraid a word would come out by itself if he didn't hold it back, and tears came down his face like crazy.

"Oh, jesus, I'm sorry. Mama'd never do that. Mama'd never do that." If he'd been bigger I'd have told him how much trouble I'd be in at the next checkpoint if I didn't have the kids registered to me. Truck's not much, but jail's worse. Or I might have tried to explain I love my babies and everything I was doing was for them as much as me.

Instead I rocked him until he fell asleep in my lap, while Cilehe cried herself out.

When the truck pulled over the black truck was there. We parked, I jumped out and Cal was waiting. "Got something for you," he said to Tomi, and from behind his back he pulled out a big bag of M&M's. "Can you share those with your little sister?"

I shot him a look. It was an awful lot of candy. But Tomi was so excited I could hardly take it away from him. Cal took Tomi's other hand and we all went into the stop.

"Why don't we grab a couple of burgers and eat in your truck?" Cal said.

"Sure." I explained to Tomi that Mama'd be gone for a while, but was coming back. "Be brave for Cilehe," I said.

Cal messed with those switches again while I wolfed down my cheeseburger. You can get really horny again in just a few hours, especially when it's been almost three years since the time before.

He lay with his head on my stomach. "You've really got nice kids," he said.

"Thanks."

"Do they look like their fathers?"

"Actually, I think they favor me more. Too bad for them."

"I don't have any complaints," he said quietly, drawing his hand along the bottom of my jaw.

I felt I was blushing, though I'm a little dark for that. "Go on."

"Your boy's a real little man. What's his name again?"

"Tomi."

"Tomi, right. I hope Jess grows up like that."

"I'm sure he will."

"Do your kids get along well?"

"Sure. Tomi's a great big brother. Kids can get to feel responsible for each other sometimes."

"Do you think so?"

I laughed. "When they aren't trying to kill each other. But I'm glad they have each other. I never had any sisters or brothers. My mama got some kind of infection in her tubes that stopped her from having more babies. I'm sorry about that sometimes."

"But you had friends, other kids you grew up with."

"Yeah."

He looked away. "Jess will never have a sister. He's never spent more than an hour in the company of the same children."

I brushed back the little pieces of hair around his forehead with my fingers. "I'm sorry."

"There's nothing you can do about it." Then he looked straight up at me, his light brown eyes real intense. "Except maybe there is."

"What do you mean?"

"Loan me one of your kids."

"What?"

He pulled himself up out of my lap and took my shoulders. "Let one of your kids ride in my truck for a leg or two. To play with Jess. To get to know him, and be a big brother or sister to him."

I shook his hands off. "That's crazy, Cal! You can't take off with my baby. I might never see you again!"

He patted his hand on the little hidden panel. "I told you we'd see each other again before, and how did it turn out?"

"But how do you know we'll even be staying on the same route?"

"Do you think I could make those changes if I didn't have access to your central controller's data through the remote unit?"

I guessed not. Still– "What if there's a checkpoint, and I have one kid too few and you have one too many? We'd both be arrested and I don't think they'll accept your asking me so nicely as a good excuse."

"Same source of information," he said. "There's no checkpoint on this route until Utah."

All that from a little panel I hadn't even known was there. "If you can do that sort of stuff," I said, "why aren't you–"

He put a finger over my lips. "I know I seem complicated," he said. "But just look at me and you'll see how simple I really am. I thought I needed time alone to help me get over–" He stopped and looked away, then he smiled at me. "Now I know I was right." He swapped his own lips for his finger. Then after a while he leaned back and said, "As a favor to me?"

"I–"

"Or as a favor to Jess. You're a mother. You know what children need. If you help him out you'll be being the mother he never had."

This was all coming so fast. My first plan began to be pushed away by a whole different Plan B. Which wasn't a bad plan at all, since it could supply everyone's needs and make all of us happy. Another three hour's drive from now, when I saw how things were going, I'd have a pretty good idea how likely Plan B was.

"All right," I said. "For Jess's sake."

I thought the point of M&M's was not to get chocolate all over your face. Cal took a paper napkin and wiped off Cilehe's mouth, gentle and careful, and rubbed his hand through her hair just like a daddy should.

Tomi stared up at him. I realized for the first time he'd never seen a man that close before.

"Which one?" Cal asked.

I considered. "Tomi looks scared of you. How about Cilehe?"

"That's fine." He picked her up. "You're coming with me, pretty lady."

She started screaming.

"Um–I'm sorry–she's usually not like that." Well, sometimes she'll go a whole day without screaming much. I took her from him and rocked her until she shut it down. I carried her outside to the big black truck.

"I'll take her from here," Cal said, reaching for my baby.

I suddenly didn't much like the looks of that black truck. "Maybe it's not such a good idea," I said.

"Shawana," he said. He leaned forward and kissed me; while kissing me, he took Cilehe from my arms, smooth as silk. "We'll just try it for this leg. If she's unhappy, she goes straight back with you. Maybe your little boy would like to ride in such a big truck next time, huh?" He said that to Tomi, who stared up at him. "Or you might like to have Jess, later," he said to me. "I'd like you to get to know him."

"I'd like that too," I said.

He smiled. He kissed me again, and he ruffled Tomi's hair with the hand that wasn't holding Cilehe. "See you in a few hours," he said, opened his door, and swung the two of them up into the cab so fast I never got more than a glimpse of it, big and dark like the truck's outside, before the door shut. But then he rolled down the window.

"You're a really special lady, did you know?" he said.

The black truck pulled away.

Tomi started to cry.

"Don't," I said to him, "c'mon, don't cry." We went back to the truck, me pulling and pulling on Tomi's arm, him not wanting to move. "Don't cry, it's okay, everything's wonderful, listen to Mama."

After Nebraska is Colorado, which at least isn't flat all the way through. Tomi usually loves hills and mountains, going up and down. Cilehe hates having her ears pop, hates it worse when they won't pop. I had to keep reminding myself I didn't have to worry about it.

"Where's Cee, Mama? Where's Cee?"

"Just ahead of us, baby. A couple miles ahead. It's okay, baby."

"Where's Cee?" he insisted. I thought his sister could get on my nerves!

"She's fine, Tomi. Watch the TV."

"Where's Cee?"

Helping us get out of this truck, baby. Up with a man who wants a mother for his son, comfort for his bed, and once he has them won't have any reason to stay in these rolling jail cells. A man who knows enough about computers to get a job that buys stereos and big TV's with channels you can change and nice haircuts that look pretty. A man who's actually wanted to get married, and can want to again.

A man we can all live with just fine, if it means getting out of this truck.

Plan B.

I decided it was some sugar reaction thing making Tomi so cranky and it would wear down. He did get quiet after a while, after I stopped trying to answer his questions.

It seemed like the longest stretch we'd ever driven. I spent it trying out all the different ways Plan B could work. Ways to become a permanent part of Cal's life. To get out of the truck. I'd never even begun to guess what it's like in it. Some drivers even have told me they'd thought it would be a great way to get away from their mamas nagging on them all the time. Me, I didn't want to risk an illegal abortion. Some nasty nights I've wondered if I did the right thing.

Then I began to worry if I'd done the right thing having Cilehe ride with Cal. She's the cranky one. If she was kicking a shitfit, and if his Jess wasn't the cranky type so he wasn't used to it, he might get a bad impression of me as a mother. It's not my fault she's cranky. Every baby's different. But he might not know that.

When the truck started to pull over, it seemed like three hours. Hell, it seemed like six. I wanted to find out how it had gone, make a little nice with Cal, and let Tomi see his sister so he'd stop pestering me.

It wasn't until we were almost there I saw it wasn't a truck stop.

It was a checkpoint.

There wasn't supposed to be one till Utah! Cal said we were perfectly safe swapping babies until then. Cal was right about everything else—how could he have screwed this up?

There was a knock on the window. "Out of the truck, lady."

"What's this all about?" I called, thinking hard.

"Just come out of the truck, and there won't be any trouble."

There were cops out there, besides the welfare worker who usually just checks your license, makes sure you are who you say you are and your babies are okay. There were cops out there, and they had guns.

"Why do you want to have guns on me?" I called, just to use up some time and think some more.

"Come on out of the truck," the first cop repeated, but another one said, "Child abandonment's a serious charge, lady."

Oh christ yes, it is. Worst thing they can catch us at aside from welfare fraud.

"I wouldn't abandon my babies!"

"Maybe so," said the second cop, "but that's not the tip we got from the trucker who just came through."

"She was lying."

"Don't think *he* was." The cop elbowed his friend and said, "Look at her face. She knows who we're talking about."

The other one sniggered. "You can learn a lot about a girl's secrets when you get a piece of her. Maybe we should start an undercover program! I'll volunteer."

I felt like I'd been hit, but I knew I had to stay cool. "Let me get out and I'll explain."

"That's what we're asking you to do, lady—"

They give you two weeks training before they put you on the road. That's hardly enough to begin to know how to drive the truck manually, and it's a couple years since I even had that. But nobody expects us to ever really have to drive, whatever the emergency regs say.

Maybe that's why it caught them flatfooted when a driver made a break for it.

They were just about right, too.

I leaned forward and yanked the handle marked Manual Override. I hit the gas. I nearly ran over a cop and I did go right through two trees on my way to the highway. A sound of metal crumpling. I couldn't look at the road much because it took all my concentration shifting gears, trying to pick up some speed. It took all my concentration and it still sounded awful. I wondered if I was stripping gears. I wondered if I could do anything wrong that would crash the truck.

He set me up. He stole my baby and he set me up. Why would he steal my baby?

I leaned hard on my horn. A big RV just got out of my way in time.

He must have known the checkpoint was coming up. And you need at least one kid to be a trucker. If there was no little Jess, he needed a baby. If he could alter his trucking card, make it look like Cilehe was his, then his only problem was me telling them at the same checkpoint I didn't have my other baby because he took her from me. I'd still be in big trouble, but so would he. And with almost no other guys in the trucks, he'd be easy to track down.

(I was afraid I really gave him Cilehe because I was tired of dealing with her fussing all the time. I never asked to be a mother, but I was one–the worst who ever lived–)

Cars were scattering in front of me. Horns blaring. Out of the corner of my eye I suddenly saw Tomi had climbed up the wall of his playpen to look out at what was going on.

"Get down, Tomi! Get down!" I grabbed out with my right hand and yanked him hard down on the playpen's mattress. The truck lurched. He went spinning across and hit his head on the other pen wall. The walls are light. I could see it give.

I couldn't look to see if he was okay. I had to keep changing lanes while I went faster.

That bastard made sure they wouldn't listen to me. He told them I was a child abandoner, so then anything I said would sound like a lie, to save my ass. He went on the offensive before I had a chance.

I started to hear sirens.

I went faster. I was almost to top gear, driving on the shoulder because it was too hard to keep going around the cars.

Thank god we were on a flattish stretch.

All the time I thought Cal was someone I could marry to get me and my babies out of the truck, even feeling guilty because I enjoyed his body but I wasn't likely to love him back–all that time he was setting me up.

I realized I was swearing, fast and steady in a low fierce voice. Tomi whimpered. At least he was awake.

"You damn black truck you fucker where are you you son of a bitch you fucker you stole my baby you bastard you lied to me!"

Lights began flashing in my side mirrors. The cops were catching up. I had to catch him before they caught me.

I shifted up. I was almost at top gear.

A couple cars split in front of me, screeching out of the way, and there was the bastard. He was going uphill. Black smoke belched out of a side pipe. I hit the foot of the hill and I remembered I had to downshift, fast. The truck couldn't keep that speed climbing. I made myself do it though I just wanted to go faster and faster until I had him–

The truck made horrible noises. I wasn't in the right gear. I slowed and started to lose ground. He must've seen me by now. I shifted, shifted, shifted until it didn't make those awful noises. I didn't care if my truck was trashed—shit, I'd be in prison anyway, my babies god knows where—but I wasn't going to lose that black monster truck.

He hit the top of the hill and vanished from sight. I got there minutes later—I say minutes, but it must have been five seconds. His truck was picking up speed fast. Mine plunged down while my stomach stayed back up top. Tomi wailed. I shifted up and up and shoved the gas to the floor. I was gaining on him. The lights were close in the side mirrors.

I could make out the face of the nearest cop, he was that close. Could see his little blond moustache, even, and the mean way he looked like he was going to kill me if I didn't do it for him first.

A red sports car was half an inch in front of me, getting closer. I had to hit the brakes, and the engine almost died. Almost. I was hitting on the gearshifter like it was Cal's face, kicking the accelerator like it was his balls.

The black truck ducked ahead of a blue minivan. The van hit its brakes hard and seemed to come right back into me, like Cal had thrown it into my face deliberately.

I swerved. I missed it.

I spent long seconds wrestling with the wheel.

Looked up and saw him cut again in front of some foreign-looking job.

He didn't have it figured right. He was going to plow right into a station wagon in the next lane by the shoulder—

"Cilehe!" I screamed. I hit my horn. I careened on the shoulder as he careened off it.

There was a steep hill a few yards off the side of the shoulder, and the black truck was about to go straight down it—

I grabbed Tomi, hit the gas hard, and shut my eyes.

The whole world went white.

It shouldn't have worked. I couldn't see, because the airbags came bursting out and filled my face with canvas.

My truck caught his trailer right on the side, smashed into it and spun his truck around almost facing behind us. I went mostly straight, destroying my cab but not quite me or Tomi, cushioned in airbag. I had a concussion, though.

The black truck came to a stop angled over the side of the hill. But it didn't roll down.

When the cops helped me out of what was left of my cab, I could hardly see straight. I did see that the black truck's trailer had burst open. I saw broken crates. I saw the ugly black metal shapes inside them. And, thank god, I didn't see Cal. If I'd seen him I don't know what I would have done to him, concussion and all.

I screamed until they put Cilehe in my arms. She was so quiet and good you'd swear she was her brother.

I had time to think in the hospital. When my head cleared—before then, if you believe the nurses—I demanded they run the tests. It was the biggest relief of my life to learn Plan A hadn't worked. A little bit of Cal growing inside me is the last thing I wanted. I know a baby has nothing to do with his daddy. I'm sure no Shawn Parker. But I wanted no piece of Cal. The plan to have three kids so they'd let me out seems like a foolish, childish thing now.

I made them tell me about Cal. They acted like I had no right to know, but they gave in enough to tell me that his real name was Charles Kavey, he was single and had assets of over a million, and was—surprise—no welfare trucker. He worked with his controller, and they made, said the government lawyer type, "illicit shipments."

I bet. I don't know anything about high-tech weapons, but I guess I can tell the ugly things when I see them. Interstate 80 could've taken him on to San Francisco, and from there I imagine they could have been smuggled either down to Chile or to the civil war in the Philippines. (News comes on twice a day in the truck, though I always wonder what they're leaving out of it.)

Cal—Charles—and his buddy must have had the system pretty well bamboozled, all the parts that are just computer talking to computer; but when it comes to the checkpoints, human beings make sure your babies match up with what it says on the license. No way around needing a real live kid for that. I guess when he found out about the surprise checkpoint, he was already on the road. He had it down so smooth, he must have used his little trick for getting a kid before. I couldn't even have identified him, if it had ever come to that. He didn't have the braid when he got to the checkpoint—it actually came off somehow, which surprised the hell out of me—and his hair was black and his eyes were dark blue. Contacts and dye. He was real smooth. The bastard enjoyed it too, I bet. Bastard.

He'd had to perform his act on short notice—unless it was a dream when I heard the nurses gossiping. When I did dream after that, the dreams were full of nightmares about a shriveled-up dead baby boy jammed in a carton among all the weapons in the black truck's trailer.

Probably the baby's name wasn't even really Jess. . . .

My grandma called the hospital. She wanted to know if she could help. She's got so little I hated to ask her, but I did.

After all, I'm back in the truck as soon as the hospital releases me, and I don't want to stay there.

But if I don't eat desserts, don't buy new clothes and makeup for myself, and take what my grandma can give me, I can start studying. Kimberlea manages; so can I. Even with my allowance cut in half in penalty for smashing up the truck. I can read really good. I'm going to take Kimberlea for a role model and order myself some accounting textbooks. Maybe even, years from now, when I'm out and I've gotten used to computers, I can go on studying and get a truck controller's license.

Nobody's going to make me keep doing what they want me to do.

My babies are going to be proud of their mama.

Dog's Life

"You're *what?*" asked Angela.

Herb, a large, dusty-beige dog, sat beside a cardboard box that contained the few items—a bone, a catnip mouse, a couple of worn blankets—that the animals agreed they could rightfully claim as theirs. The Siamese, Wayfarer, lay curled atop it.

"We're moving out," Herb said. Wayfarer gave a triumphant flick of her tail.

"But why?"

"Animals," said Martin. "Don't have an ounce of gratitude."

"*Gratitude*," Wayfarer sneered. "Gratitude for being locked up in this dingy house when there are cats out there I have a right to see? Gratitude for being fed brown sludge from a can? Gratitude, I imagine, for being thrown bodily out of any chair I happen to be napping in if some human being wants it instead?"

"So who bought that chair? Who bought that food?"

"Martin," said Angela, warningly. She turned to the animals. "Wayfarer, Herb, I'm sure we can work this out. Let's talk about this."

"The time for talking is through. What reason is there for four-footed animals to be subservient to two-footed? It's slavery," she said cooly, her tail describing a figure eight in the air.

"Do you feel that way too?" Angela asked the dog.

Herb looked away. "I think she's right," he said, "that there's something wrong about living like this. I'm sorry."

"Oh, Herb—"

"No hard feelings," the dog said gruffly. He nosed the box forward. Angela looked at him helplessly. "Um, could I trouble you to open the door?"

"Be my *guest*," Martin said, yanking it open with an obsequious gesture out. Angela reached out a hand to stroke the dog's ear, but pulled it back, watching as Wayfarer rode the carton of worldly possessions Herb pushed down the street.

"We should have thought this out more," Wayfarer complained.

We? thought Herb, since it all had been the cat's idea, but he kept it to himself. Instead he pulled the blankets out of the box and arranged them as best he could behind a dumpster. Shivering in the autumn chill, he tried to sleep, Wayfarer providing the only spot of warmth where she pressed against his flank.

At dawn Herb woke from a fitful doze to find a ragged, spotted mongrel sniffing at him. "Morning," said the strange dog. "What's a couple pets like you doing out on the street?"

"How d'you know?" Herb mumbled.

"Hmm what?"

"How can you tell we're pets?"

The mongrel looked amused. "Collars," he said.

"Oh," said Herb.

"So?" said the spotted dog. Wayfarer gave a sleeping snort and rolled over. "What happened–kicked out?"

"No–our decision."

The mongrel shook his head. "Pretty dumb. You gave up a roof and a meal ticket to eat out of garbage cans?"

Herb had been considering that, but he drew himself up–trying not to wake the cat–and said, stiffly, "We declared independence. It's a political statement. Humans and dogs–and cats–can't relate honestly until we meet on an equal level." He strained his head around, chewed at his loose collar, tore it off and flung it to the asphalt.

"Wow," said the mongrel. "No kidding? Then you got guts, kid."

Herb doubted it, but it felt good to hear. "Thanks."

"Maybe not brains, though." Herb blinked. "Incidentally, this is my alley. Find yourself other crashspace tomorrow night." The spotted dog made a quick deposit against the brick wall and trotted off.

"Tuna?" murmured Wayfarer in her sleep. "No, I'll have the salmon mousse."

o o o

Herb could—just barely—make himself root through a garbage can and pretend it was table scraps, but Wayfarer always demanded the best of whatever he found. "Siamese have delicate digestions," she said primly in a voice that allowed no argument.

It wasn't the food that bothered Herb, or trying to sleep without freezing or being run off by former occupants. He felt like a deadbeat.

"I need time to recover from my deep-rooted trauma," Wayfarer said when he brought it up. "Anyway, if we're really declaring independence from an inequitable system, there's no reason to play by its rules."

Herb was stubborn. Leaving Angela and Martin to be his own dog meant assuming his own responsibilities. And winter was coming on.

"You gotta be kidding," said the security chief.

"Please, sir," said Herb. "You're the first employer I've been able to get through to. Give me a chance."

"Canines ain't independents," said the chief. "Ain't done."

"I'll work cheap. I'll earn any responsibility you give me."

"How cheap?"

"Less than minimum wage," Herb offered desperately. "I'm not a human—it's legal."

"True," said the chief.

"And you can get rid of me if you aren't satisfied. I don't have a union and I don't need a contract."

"Good, 'cause I don't sign contracts with mutts."

Wayfarer expressed disappointment at his joining the system; but didn't reject the one-room, no bath apartment Herb found. The landlady looked dubious, but took the cash. "Just till I get real people for it." With what she charged for the dingy hole, that was as unlikely as the animals' getting an actual lease. Still, there was money left over for Herb to buy generic dry dog food, and the expensive single-serving food and occasional fresh fish Wayfarer demanded for her digestion.

Herb suggested the cat try to clean the place up while he was at work. Somehow it seemed he ended up doing most of the heavy work.

"You're much better suited for it," she commented, grooming her whiskers.

"What does that mean?" he demanded, losing his patience.

"You're bigger—you're stronger—you have a better constitution. And you're more temperamentally suited to unimaginative work."

He struggled to remind himself they were fellow oppressed creatures, and nothing could come without a little sacrifice.

And he did enjoy the pride he felt, supporting himself, beholden to no one. He liked working for a living.

"Sorry," said the chief. "This came outta management. Not my idea."

"But I've worked hard! I've never missed a day! I'm the best guard at the factory—canine or human!"

"I wouldn't say that was wrong. But it ain't the point."

"Look," said Herb. "I don't even know where that came from." The human-interest section between them bore the headline: "ANIMAL RIGHTS?" and the subhead, "TWO 'DECLARE INDEPENDENCE' FROM HUMANITY." There was a picture of Wayfarer looking soberly into the distance, head raised nobly. There was also a small, fuzzy old shot of himself leaping for a frisbee, one of the few mementos Herb had brought from Angela's house. "I never talked to any reporters."

"It's lousy publicity for the company. We don't need trouble."

Herb got home before dawn to find a box on the sidewalk in front of their building. On the box was Wayfarer. Her tail blurred with motion.

"That rotten—*human*," she said, and hissed. "She's evicted us! Said she runs a quiet building. Hah! *That's* a joke. Where is she at three a.m. when all the radios are blasting?"

Herb dropped the moist newspaper in front of Wayfarer. "What do you know about this?" he asked her.

Wayfarer glanced at it. "Oh, that. The picture's not too bad, is it? I think my other side is better."

"Did you talk to that reporter?"

"Why not? I've got nothing else to do all day," Wayfarer said. "This neighborhood doesn't have a very good class of cats," she added critically.

"It got me fired!" Herb said. "Don't you think you could have consulted with me first?"

The cat stared at him. "You don't own me," she said coldly. "Did I escape the domination of human beings to take orders from a dog?"

"I'm sorry," Herb said awkwardly.

"All right, I'll accept that. What's for dinner?"

Wayfarer refused to sleep on the street again. Herb had exactly $27. The place they found wanted ten dollars a night for a room that made their previous quarters look palatial; Herb had a piece of work talking Wayfarer into accepting the room. "We can't afford anything better. We can only pay for two nights as it is."

"So get another job," she said.

Most places still outright refused to talk to a dog. Others glared. "You're that troublemaker, aren't you?" Word seemed to have gotten to all the firms that used guard dogs, and he couldn't think of other work to try for.

The second day was worse. Street animals were no friendlier than the humans. "Life's rough enough without muzzy-headed idealists like you rocking the boat!" a little three-legged terrier called angrily at him. And there were no jobs available, not even interviews.

Dejected, he walked back to the hotel, five dollars in his pouch.

Wayfarer was not alone. "Mr. Herb Canis, I presume?" the man with the briefcase said, extending a hand.

"Canis?" said Herb. He shook hands, which made him feel vaguely ridiculous, as though he were rolling over. A card appeared in the man's hand and Herb took it in his mouth.

"Canis," said Wayfarer. "We can hardly go by Norlander, can we? Names are identity, the selves we show the world. —And 'Wayfarer Norlander' sounds ridiculous. I considered changing 'Wayfarer,' but I've dignified that name by making it my own, and taken 'Felis' for a surname, as an example to felines everywhere."

"She has quite a message, doesn't she?" said the man. "And the style and conviction to get it across."

"This isn't another reporter, is it?" asked Herb. "Wayfarer, we've had enough trouble."

"Hardly," said the man, with a polite little laugh. "If you'd look at my card—"

Herb dropped it on the floor and read "Foster Roderick, Flair Public Relations."

"I have engaged Ms. Felis on Oprah and Donahue, and I'm working on Letterman." Wayfarer stretched contentedly on the satin cushion Herb had bought her with his first paycheck.

"What? So fast?"

Roderick said, "I had the bookings yesterday evening. The only catch was finding Ms. Felis and yourself—you see what a good p.r. firm can accomplish. Getting you to the top will be trivial by comparison."

"Us?"

"I speak of you as compatriots, of course. You do realize, though, that it's Ms. Felis—"

"You may call me Wayfarer, Foster," she purred.

"Wayfarer has a quality. She'll be beautifully telegenic. She'll just leap from the screen." He looked Herb over. "You—well, you have a certain blue-collar charm, I'd say. We might be able to do something with you later. But let's start with Wayfarer, don't you think?"

"Sure," said Herb, dazed.

A limo picked Wayfarer up for her first interview. A limo drove them, days later, to their new Michigan Avenue condo. Wayfarer jetted around the country, and Herb stayed home and watched her on television.

The networks ran stories covering pet-store picketings, Wayfarer providing commentary. Animal rights bills were introduced. Shelters for street animals and disaffected pets sprang up. Wayfarer t-shirts flooded department stores, one of the many rights to her image Roderick had sold.

Herb had nothing to do.

He slipped out of the building one day and took himself for a walk. He was a little concerned he'd be recognized as Wayfarer's partner, but he wasn't. He walked for an hour before he realized he was headed for the office where Angela worked. No big deal, he told himself; the odds of running into anyone downtown are tiny.

So it took three hours before Angela walked down the street.

She drew up short and looked at him. Finally she said, "Herb."

"Hi."

"So, um, what are you doing downtown?"

"Nothing much. Window shopping."

"Okay." There was an awkward silence.

"Hey, um, I know what Wayfarer's been saying about you and Martin on TV. I just want you to know those are her opinions, not mine."

"Sure," said Angela. "The enemy always has to be made out to be a monster to get the fight going. I know."

"Well, I know it can't have made things easy for you two."

"Herb," she said. "Maybe you—should know Martin and I split up."

"Why?" he asked, surprised.

"Oh, you know, he wasn't the most sensitive guy in the world. House got awfully quiet after. . . ." She trailed off.

"Yeah."

"You wouldn't want to move back?" she asked suddenly.

"Oh, gosh, Angela, that's really nice of you, but—"

"I'm sorry. It was a stupid question."

"It just wouldn't be right."

"Sure," said Angela. Dog and woman stared at each other. "Look, I'd better get going. We'll get together sometime, all right?"

"Sure," said Herb.

The Loop was crowded with humans. Herb found himself retreating to the alleys. He didn't feel like going back to the empty condo, not even with all the plush cushions scattered through all the rooms and the fabulously stocked kitchen. Not a one of those cushions, he thought, silk or satin or velvet, was as comfortable as the beat-up old armchair Angela kept in the den for him.

Did I ask to be a symbol? he thought. Maybe he did. You have to be awful careful in this life. He sat down by a dumpster to ponder.

"Hey, this is my turf," growled a voice. Herb looked up and the voice became warmer. "Oh, it's you. Herb, right?"

"Yes," he confirmed to the spotted mongrel.

"Didn't guess I was talking to future celebrities, way back when. Guess you were smarter than I thought."

"Maybe not," Herb said morosely.

"What's your problem? You got fame and fortune without doing squat. That snotty little cat friend of yours does it all."

"I don't think she minds," Herb said.

"Going on Carson and eating caviar? No, probably not. Just like a cat." The mongrel paused, then allowed, "Well, maybe not all of them."

"It's like Wayfarer, though, I guess. But it's for a good cause," Herb said defensively. "It calls attention to social problems. She's living a very fulfilling life."

"You're not?" the mongrel asked. "Christ, you've got all the money in the world. You can eat anything you want. You don't need to keep fighting folks out of your sleeping space. Sounds great to me."

"I hate it!" Herb cried. "I don't *do* anything. I was working before, and that was better."

"So get a job."

"I'm kind of too famous to be a watchdog now. What else can I do?"

"Get into investments. Real estate—that's always good," the spotted dog said sagely. He cocked an eye. "You don't look excited."

"It's—" Herb paused. "I don't know how to say this. I liked the way I lived before."

"Ah," said the mongrel.

"I ran into my old mistress today, and she invited me back. But I can't do that. I'll be known as a Fido! I couldn't live with myself either, if I backed down from a moral decision."

"Yep."

"So what should I do?"

"How the hell do I know?" said the mongrel. "I got problems of my own. And unless you got some food to share, I got business."

"Thanks a lot," Herb said to the empty alley.

"You want a job?" Wayfarer said. "No problem. Why didn't you say something before?"

"When were you around to talk to?"

"We can arrange something. Let me see—there've been some threats recently. We can find room for Herb with the bodyguards, can't we, Foster?" she said to the manager, interrupting his phone call.

"Mmm? Oh, sure."

"How's that, Herb? Put Herb on the payroll, Foster."

The manager jotted a note.

"One other thing, Wayfarer."

"Could you make it fast? My personal groomer will be here soon."

"I'd like to invest some of the money."

Foster Roderick looked up. "Ms. Felis's money?"

"I thought this was a partnership."

"Certainly any 'partnership'—of which there is no legal existence—is more than fulfilled by your excellent room and board here."

Herb took a deep breath. "I supported Wayfarer—"

Roderick snorted. "Hardly at this level!"

"And whether or not there's anything legal, I think—"

"I have to protect Ms. Felis's interests—"

The buzzer sounded. "That's my groomer," said Wayfarer stiffly.

"Of course," said Herb. He rose with great dignity.

"He probably wouldn't cost that much to buy off," he heard Wayfarer tell Roderick as the door swung shut behind him.

So he became one of Wayfarer's personal bodyguards. He followed her around and stared at anyone who got too close. Wayfarer didn't like anyone to get too close.

When she traveled, humans, not Herb, traveled with her. When Wayfarer was on a lecture circuit out of Chicago, he studied how to invest the little parcel of money she had allowed him, shopping rental properties and studying commodities.

He felt a little better. But still lonely.

One of Wayfarer's bodyguards broke his leg two hours before a flight, with no time to replace him. "You don't mind, do you, Herb?"

Not only had Herb never been on an airplane, he had never dreamed of flying first class. He was nervous about flying, but excited.

Wayfarer said he was to board to check out the cabin. They were late to the airport, and there was some confusion, until Roderick explained the situation to the boarding attendant.

The first class cabin was nearly full, the flight attendants preoc-
cupied with a screaming set of triplets in back, and Herb didn't know
how to find his seat. He turned to a matronly woman sitting on the
aisle. "Pardon me, ma'am, could you–"

The woman shrieked. "My god, a wolf!"

The man sitting behind her said, "Calm down. It's only a mangy
dog. Stewardess! Stewardess, a dog has wandered onto the plane."

"Get that thing out of here," someone else said. "I'm allergic. I
paid good money to have a good seat on this plane. What is this airline coming to? I'm writing a letter!"

"No, I have a–ouch!" The allergic man had swatted him with the
inflight magazine. Herb's ticket fell from his pouch and was trampled.

Wayfarer strolled onto the plane. "Herb, what is going on here?"

The matronly woman turned. "Oh, my, you're–you're–you're
that famous one, aren't you? I have your book in my purse!"

"Wayfarer Felis," supplied the allergic man.

"This is terrible," the woman said. "A celebrity on board and this
scruffy beast causing trouble! He could eat her! I'll complain to the
airline for you, dear. You will autograph my book, won't you?"

"That dog is my traveling companion," Wayfarer said.

"Oh–my–"

"I can see I have a long way to go in my mission to bring animals
to full legal stature." Everyone looked respectfully chastened.

A steward hurried up, Herb's ticket was found and he was seated
beside Wayfarer with many apologies. Wayfarer looked coldly at
him. "You should have handled it," she hissed under her breath, then
smiled at the matronly woman and autographed her book with a
pawprint.

There was caviar for Wayfarer. The flight attendants were polite,
even deferential, to Herb, but it seemed everyone wanted to pretend
he didn't exist. Wayfarer didn't say another word to him.

Herb resigned before she could fire him. He talked to a lawyer,
who talked to Roderick; a week later, he put his pawprint on a
release from any future demands on Wayfarer, and took the check
she wrote him in return without a word.

o o o

Managing a six-unit apartment building was hard work. On a typical day he might take a shoulder to Mrs. Fox's stuck window, vacuum the front steps with the vacuum hose in his mouth, drain the muck from the hot water heater, mediate a dispute between across-the-hall neighbors, grant the young dance student a week extension on her rent, take out the trash and call the plumber about the Prokopiaks's toilet. The roach problem would be getting worse again, the neighborhood kids throwing beer bottles on the front lawn, and the gutters developing a leak.

He was exhausted. He was deeply satisfied.

And every night at 11:30, he would look both ways, sneak up the stairs and across the hall to apartment 2-B, and snuggle under the blankets at the feet of his tenant—Angela Norlander.

It was a dog's life. He could deal with it.

The Arbitrary
Placement of Walls

The trip to the kitchen like this:

Stand up from the folding chair six feet to the left of the far corner of the living room. Wide circle around the red armchair. The television is on. It makes a lot of noise. Basketball. Laura doesn't know anything about basketball; the confusion of the game comforts her a little.

Crossing the living-room floor in four big steps. A wide semi-circle, to avoid the coffee table. She replaced the coffee table a year ago, but it didn't make any difference. She'd known it wouldn't.

Up the hall: left side, left side, right side, left side, right side, right side, right side, left side. A whispering at the fourth step. It can't be helped.

Dining room best ignored. Past the back bedroom, which is best ignored too: more whispers, many whispers; she tightens her inner ears to make a roar to drown them out. Finally into the kitchen. The thin blue line on the linoleum around the stove is one of the first she painted. There used also to be ribbons, ropes, strings around corners and chairs and places, different colors, color-coded. She's taken them down. Sometimes she can't keep intruders out of the apartment, and anyway she knows where all the ghosts are now. She steps around the line to the refrigerator. Takes a Pepsi and pops it open. She likes Coke. So did Eric.

She looks at the line around the stove and wonders how much acetone it would take to remove it. Maybe she could just paint lines around the refrigerator, the microwave stand, the kitchen table. Make it look like a Statement.

Thinking about Statements she missteps her way past the stove, stepping on the line. Blue ghosts. Donald memories. Donald frying bacon, naked, dancing away from the sizzles. She remembers yelling at him not to be an idiot, laughing at him. She has long since forgotten exactly what she said. Donald is always there to say what he said.

"It takes a real man to brave elemental fire for his woman," Donald says. Pauses, listening. Dusting of bright blond hair down his belly. "You think I'm afraid of a little bit of grease?"

"You should be, jerk," Laura says into the unresponsive air. "I only wish you'd cauterized your favorite parts." But she can't make herself sound as hostile as she wants.

"Yes I'm crazy and I love you too," Donald says. Suddenly–her memory times it perfectly–he yelps, clutches his buttock, leaps. "My god, I'm hit!" Pause. He laughs. Turns down the burner. "That's right. Kiss it and make it better–" He's collapsing in laughter. Kissing.

The Pepsi jerks in her hand, spraying Laura with sticky cold cola. She's squeezed a dented waistline around its middle. She breaks away from the blue Donald zone, wiping her hand jerkily on her jeans.

Back down the hall: right, left, left, left, right, left, right, right.

She sits two-thirds from the left side of the sofa and stares at the television screen, sipping too-sweet Pepsi. Michael Jordan leaps and spins. She tries to pay attention to the announcers, pick up the subtleties of the game. Donald taught her football, Frank taught her hockey, she taught *Eric* baseball. Basketball's new. Hers.

The doorbell rings. If it's a meter reader, he can wait for the Martins upstairs to answer. If it's not a meter reader, it's a Jehovah's Witness and child. She doesn't have visitors.

"Laura, I know you're in there. I saw you through the curtains."

Damn it. Life is complicated enough. She takes a wide arc to the front door, backtracking once as she nears Frank. She opens the apartment door to the lobby, crosses the narrow lobby space in two steps and peers through the front door peephole. If she squints down angled from the left she can barely see through it. Not Eric and three dozen roses. She sees her mother, two plastic grocery bags dragging down her arm.

What to do? Laura closes her eyes and opens the door.

"I'm not feeling very–" she begins, but her mother, a stout energetic woman in a perm Laura hasn't seen before, is already in the lobby. "You keep saying you'll come for dinner and you never do," her mother says. "So I have a nice chicken from the Jewel"–lifting one bag–"and a little something to drink with it"–lifting the other. "No arguing now. You let me in your kitchen and I'll have it in the oven in a flash. Then we can chat while it cooks."

Furious thought. "That's so much work, Mother. Let me take you out to a restaurant."

"Don't be ridiculous. I could do a chicken in my sleep, after forty years of it. What are you eating, that terrible microwave food? You could let your mother make you a real meal once a year besides Thanksgiving."

No way out. As she crosses the worn tiles of the lobby her mother's sturdy pink-sneakered foot squeals on the ceramic. In a flash Frank is solidly between them, jogging in place, his running shoes squeaking. "You look fine already, why jog so much?" she asked, four years ago.

Frank grins and gathers up a nonexistent love handle under his t-shirt. "When this body is perfect, your highness, then you'll really be in my power." He leans forward for a kiss, misses, stumbles, his new shoes squealing again. "See? Not irresistible yet. But soon–soon you'll be begging–and then *I'll* laugh–" and chortling, mock-sinister, he turns and runs out the door through her mother. Goodbye again, Frank.

"Laura?" She jumps. "I swear, you're always daydreaming, honey. Are we going in, or do we stand in the lobby all day?"

"I'm sorry, Mother. I've been feeling a little tired." A fumble with the key. Her stomach hollows as she sees her mother seeing the place, realizes what it looks like through orderly, domestic eyes. Christ. What a mess it is: old newspapers piled at apparent haphazard to block off bad places, traces of old chalk outlines lingering in worn carpet which hasn't been vacuumed in months, furniture in odd places–sofa in a corner, television on the mantelpiece, chairs angled erratically, the big red armchair near the center of the floor.

"Have you been sick? It looks like you haven't cleaned in ages. Is the whole place like this?"

A tally of bad places and the arbitrary placement of walls around them: living room, sunporch, big bedroom, little bedroom, study (the barest, least comfortable room, where she sleeps on a sprung mattress retrieved from someone's trash), the bathroom, and the lobby whose floor she hasn't mopped or even swept–"I'm afraid I've done better. We're busy at work. A lot of overtime." She grabs the red armchair and wrestles it to the nearest corner, its former corner, so mortified she barely sees the kaleidoscope of ghosts she plows through in the process. Back in place, Eric snores softly once, curled in red velvet, rubs his eyes, smiles sleepily up at her, murmurs: "Love you, Lauracakes. . . ."

She whirls away. "Really it's not usually like this at all–"

"I hope not, honey. You'll make yourself sick living like this." Her mother shoves her sleeves up her sturdy arms. "That's it, then. We're going to give this place its spring cleaning. I've got the whole evening free."

The whole evening? Dear God, Laura thinks. "I don't," she lies. "I have to go out and run some errands."

"Then don't let me stop you." Her mother is already gathering up newspapers. "You just leave me here and you'll see how much better this place looks when you get back."

"No, you can't–"

"Don't argue with your mother. What would your grandparents have said, if they knew you'd let their home get like this?" She is unstoppable. Laura can't leave her alone here.

So the whole evening it is, three solid hours caught helplessly in a domestic whirlwind, in the wake of a cheerful blur of activity. Her mother digs up brooms, vacuum cleaner, garbage bags, and Laura follows unable to defend her fortresses of boxes, paper and carefully positioned furniture from being torn down and restructured into normal and deadly order. Her mother knows where everything used to be. She helped Laura move here from the dorm, years back, in the first place.

A helpless accomplice in the destruction of her wards, if Laura tries to move a chair back from a danger spot, she comes face to face with Donald Frank Eric and must retreat to hold bags for her mother's disposal of Pepsi cans, or to sweep furiously, staring at the floor where she can see only feet. Air fills with dust. Windows fling open. Nothing stops the juggernaut. It's a sickening feeling, like being dragged carelessly, at great speed, at the end of a tether across slick and dangerous ice. All she can do is pray for it to stop.

Suddenly she is taken by the shoulder and plunked into the sofa, a sweaty cold bottle shoved into her hand. "All done! That wasn't too bad, was it?" Her mother produces another bottle of wine cooler –Laura hasn't had alcohol since Eric–twisting the top off. Her mother sits in the red armchair and, though Laura sits six feet away, she can faintly see Eric sleepily stir and smile, sitting up until his curling lips are inches out of synch with her mother's. A swing band, her mother's cleaning music from the stereo, drowns out his loving murmurs. Her mother pours herself some wine cooler. The smell of roasting chicken drifts from the kitchen.

Laura takes a long pull from her bottle, gets hold of herself. The thin bite of alcohol unfamiliar on her tongue.

"I hope you like this brand, dear." She sips. "Nothing tastes better than a cold drink after a good day's cleaning."

Nothing hurts like old happiness, trapping her.

"You should be more careful with the things people leave you. Your grandparents willed you this building because they loved you, honey. You should treat it better."

"It's so big for one person," Laura says. "There's so much to do. If the Martins upstairs didn't do the yardwork, I don't know how I'd keep up."

"Then sell it," her mother says. "It would break your grandparents' hearts–but I suppose they're not around to know it."

"I can't." There are so many reasons, worn around the edges: the repairs it would need before she could put it on the market, the time it would take up, the Martins who were old friends of her grandparents and would never get such a low rent rate from any new landlord. What kind of person would put the Martins out on the street?

And no money at all to make the sort of repairs the place would need, even to cover the building's age with a bright coat of paint. Donald's investments saw to that; eternally, back in the study, he explains the columns of figures that prove his cousin's novelty factory will triple her money, give them enough for a honeymoon in Switzerland. He believed it. Any time she cares to look in the study she can see the excitement in his eyes. She saw it, unwillingly, an hour ago. She is still paying back the debts.

"Whatever you think is best," her mother says. Covering her mouth, she yawns with Eric. "Excuse me! All this exercise." She deftly rebuttons her sleeves. "I haven't moved so much furniture in years.

I used to do it all the time, you know, whenever I was really upset about something. When we couldn't pay the bills, or when your father and I fought, or when you went away to college and I missed you so much, dear. I'd just roll up my sleeves and move the furniture all around. It really gets rid of the ghosts."

Laura starts. "Ghosts?"

"Oh, you know, all those stupid old memories. It does help to keep busy. Anyway, now we can sit and catch up."

Her mother sits, pleasantly waiting for news. Laura can't think of anything to say.

"So, are you dating anybody?"

"No," she says.

"Oh, honey. Now I know I'm not supposed to push for grand-children, and I'd never do that. But don't you think you're working too hard? It couldn't hurt you to get out now and then. Aren't there any nice young men where you work?"

"They're all married."

"Oh, that's too bad. You know, I thought it was such a shame when that Eric moved to Wisconsin. He was such a sweet boy. Do you know he phoned me the other day?"

Oh Christ. Eric sits up sleepily through her mother and rubs his eyes. Her mother always liked him. Everybody liked him. He was good at that. After Donald and Frank, she hadn't been able to trust anyone, not until nice sweet Eric, polite to mothers, wonderful lis-tener, gentle in bed. The bastard. She looks away from his smiling murmurs.

"He didn't sound like himself. He's in the hospital up there, poor boy."

"The hospital? Why?"

"He wouldn't say. He said it wasn't anything important, but you know he really didn't sound so good. Hasn't he called you? Maybe you should call him. I'll give you his number." She takes her little address book and a notepad from her purse and starts to copy a list-ing.

I'll never talk to him, Laura thinks. Then she thinks: AIDS, the bastard gave me AIDS and ran out, oh Jesus.

"Here you are, honey. I never did understand what happened between you two. If he's not very sick maybe this is a blessing, get you two together for a talk and who knows what could happen?"

The bastard would just lie to her again. "Mother—"

"Not that I'd ever pressure you, dear. You know I'd just like you kids to be friends."

"Mother—"

The oven timer sounds. Her mother stands.

"Mother." She jumps up and grabs her mother's arm. "Mother, I can't eat now." Her mother looks startled. "You understand. It's upsetting. Not knowing. I have to call the hospital, okay?"

"He said it wasn't anything important, honey."

He lied all the time. "Don't forget your purse. We'll do this again. Thank you for everything." She propels her mother to the apartment door, through the lobby, to the building door.

"Don't forget the hospital number—"

She grabs it and shoves it in her pocket. "Thank you. I'll call. Goodbye!" The door slams in her mother's concerned face. Laura retreats three steps and shoves the inner door shut, stepping around where the end table used to keep her from Donald. She miscalculates. His bags are packed and he glowers without looking at her. "Bastard!" she screams at him. She thrashes the empty air, makes herself stop.

She stands trembling in the wreckage of her protection, tidy rational apartment with nowhere to hide. Every chair and table, bit and piece has used her mother as its agent to find its way back to sinister order. Closing in on her.

She has survived everything else. She will survive.

She will leave the slip of paper wadded in her pocket.

The chicken slowly turns to carbon in the oven.

Ghosts.

Frank lifts weights in the back room, in the corner once marked out with brown chalk. "You're a self-involved jerk," she shouts at him. "I don't know what I ever saw in you!" He clamps another weight on the bar and grins at her. "You don't think I can lift this? Ah, but you forget how you inspire me, oh beauteous one. Watch!"

"I don't *care*!" She throws her glass through him. It shatters against the wall. Frank doesn't stop grinning. The bar bends under the weights' mass as he lifts it over his head.

"What do I get for a reward?" he says, grunting the bar back down, reaching out—

On the floor against the coffee table, Donald hunches, knee-hugging, in rare tears, his only tears. His father's death. Weeping, bruise-eyed, he reaches up for comfort—

Eric is setting the dining-room table: it's roast goose, a sort of asparagus soufflé, German wine. She can almost taste it. Smiling, pleased with himself, he reaches out to pull her in to him—

The shower is horrible: her mother threw out the hose she rigged to the other side of the tub, shaking her head, telling Laura she really should call a plumber if she can't deal with shower pipes. Laura can't bathe without Donald Frank Eric swirling around her with the water. She sponges her armpits, washes her hair in the bathroom sink, not looking up to see who is shaving in the mirror—

She tries sleeping in her bed where it's been moved back. (Her mother threw out the mildewy mattress in the back room.) Donald makes love beside her. His lean torso moves slowly, sensually; sweat gleams along his smooth jaw; his broad hand reaches to stroke her hair. He whispers things she could barely hear the first time, can barely hear now. Nonsense.

She turns her back, squeezes her eyes shut. Still the indecipherable murmuring. Gets up and takes two sleeping pills, jams the pillow down hard over her ears. Can't shut out the murmurs. Even the bed seems to rock, slowly, sensually—

Sobbing with anger she drags the massive bed across the floor. It takes five long minutes to move it, gouging four broad pale lines in the floor. Her shoulders ache. Shake.

The bed away from where Donald touched a girl who used to be Laura, she still can't sleep. The house murmurs with the hundred ghosts of three living men.

Slip of paper wadded in her pocket.

The workday seems infinite when she's in the office. She thinks she hears gossip behind her back. Nobody says more than hello except her supervisor, Bob, lingering too long at her desk. His smug flirting brings bile to the back of her throat; she clenches her jaw until he moves on to the next woman. She routes forms, stacks and stacks of forms, trying to lose herself in the mindlessness of it. The routine is abysmal, the whispering unbearable, and the day goes on forever; and then she has to go home.

To each infinite, unbearable night.

Finally she calls the number on the lined paper.

Eric is putting a big box of Godiva chocolates on the end table next to the telephone, bidding for her attention with another present. The phone rings twice on the other end.

"Yes, could you tell me about your patient Eric Kennelly?"

"I can connect you."

Eric pulls away the chocolate box and points coyly to his lips.

"No, I don't want to talk to him. I just want to know how he's doing. Could you tell me what he's being treated for?" She knows it's not AIDS–Eric was too clever, too controlled to forget any precautions– but she tells herself she has to be sure. It's only sensible.

"I'm afraid that's not hospital policy, ma'am. I can connect you, if you like."

He unbuttons two buttons, pulls away the shirt from one shoulder and balances a chocolate on his pale skin.

"Ma'am?"

She hangs up.

An hour later she walks eight blocks to the car rental place and lays down her credit card.

He didn't even leave her for another woman. He'd just been killing time in Chicago until he could wangle an assistant professorship at UW. She was something to do in the meantime. Hindsight. "Do you know how many PhD's in history are working in personnel, or selling insurance, or sweeping high schools? And this isn't some podunk college, either. This is my big break!" But he never asked if she'd move north with him. And was packed and gone before she could ask him.

It's only a couple of hours drive to Madison, far too short. She has to stop at a gas station to find out where the hospital is. She circles it a couple times before she pulls in and parks near the Visitors sign.

"It's probably not visiting hours," she says to the woman at the desk. "I can leave if it's the wrong time."

"No, there's half an hour left." The woman smiles. "Who are you here to see?"

"That's okay, I have his room number." 258. She can almost feel the number, burning her hand from the wad of paper. Into the elevator, down the hall to the right nearly to the end; she faces the door. Hand on the knob. Opens it.

A wasted pale figure lies half-curled on a hospital bed. Tubes all over. It looks like nobody she's ever seen, barely like a human. The figure turns and opens Eric's gray-green eyes. "Laura. Well. What brings you by?"

The door gapes open behind her, air blowing through it, chilling her as if she's naked. She closes it carefully.

"I'll bet it's two weeks since I had a visitor." The voice is a rasping whisper, not Eric's soft tenor at all. He manages a lopsided sort of grin. "People get bored of watching a guy die. Can't blame them. Liver cancer's not a showbiz way to go."

She is silent.

"I knew you'd come eventually. You cut it close, though, hon."

She stares at him. She can't let herself feel sorry for the sweet and lying Eric who haunts her days and nights, so she mustn't make this miserable stick-figure look like any Eric at all.

Except the eyes. Hard not to look at the eyes.

"Laura? You going to say anything?" The stick-man swallows painfully. "I feel like I'm being visited by a ghost. You didn't go and beat me to the other side, did you?" He laughs briefly, coughs at greater length. "Sorry. Gallows humor. My psychiatrist tells me it's normal."

Just a stick-man, she tells herself. Something too big moves, like broken wings, inside her. All right! she thinks. Eric! Sick. Pitifully sick. But don't let him fool you again, don't let him—

"Laura?"

"Why did you call my mother? What do you want?"

The stick-man blinks Eric's eyes. "I don't know. Nothing. Whatever. It's so damn *boring*, dying. To see if you were still as uptight as you ever were. Amazing—you're even more uptight."

If she moves even an inch she'll be lost, he'll have won; in grief and sympathy and love she will do anything for him. She struggles to stand still, firm. So he'd be using her. Is that bad? Was he really just using her before?

He grins again, a parody of the smile that used to be his best feature. "It's something to do." Why did you move in with me if you just expected to leave in four months? she had asked him, desperate, as his car backed down the driveway. It was something to do, he said, and drove away.

"You never needed much reason," Laura says. She wonders if anesthetics linger in hospital air. Her heart beats slow and her body feels dull. Antiseptics must be stinging her eyes to tears. But she pushes down the crippled part inside her. Things die in hospitals.

The stick-man frowns. "Laura—"

"You knew how Donald and Frank hurt me, and you made it your little project to get me to trust you. Then you walked out." Something almost chokes her voice; she doesn't let it. "Kept things from being *boring,* I expect. I don't know. I've never been so *bored* I'd do that."

The stick-man coughs, starts to speak, coughs again. Lopsided grin. "Is that any way to talk to a dying man?"

"I don't give a shit what you do. You were the worst of the lot. I don't have a thing to say to you." She turns to leave, before the leaden anaesthetic feeling weights her feet in place, before the broken parts inside her weigh her heart down. While she can still move.

The stick-man rasps a sigh, presses his head back into his pillow. "Then why did you come all this way to see me?"

Laura stops without looking back. "No reason at all." Not good enough. She turns—his deep, gray-green eyes—and has to force her prepared words out: "Just a little friendly advice."

Deep breath: "Drop dead."

She closes the door behind her with perfect silence.

After her brilliant, cutting exit, what a shock to see Eric flush and laughing on the front stoop.

"You're dying," she tells him, and at the dining-room table, and in the red chair, and in the back bedroom, and at the kitchen sink. "Just die." Eric laughs and shows her how he can (sloppily) wash with one hand and dry with the other. All she can do is run again.

A week slides by.

Hard as she tries, she can't forget Eric dying in the hospital, too pitiful for lasting hate. To keep hate fresh she visits all the really bad ghosts. They don't hurt as much as the happy ones, the loving ones, but she's always spent less time with them.

In the back room with Donald: "If you had any sense you wouldn't have encouraged me to risk all my assets!" Mine too, she thought, but she's helpless against his hurt fury. "Flat broke and you think the wedding's still on? Give me the damn ring back and I'll at least have a thousand bucks to start a new life with." It isn't fair, but the ring clatters at his feet where she threw it at him. He picks it up without a word and stalks away; though she will wait for months for him to come to his senses, call her, apologize, he never does. Leaving her in debt, lonely, alone.

The bedroom with Frank: "I've thought about it," he says. "I'm going back to my wife." Wife? He never mentioned a wife. She would never have been stupid enough to get involved with a married man. It was his two jobs and his eternal exercise that kept his visits so erratic. "Of course I never told you I was married—we were going to get a divorce. You didn't need to know." He's pulling on his pants, not looking at her. His skin damp with sweat from their lovemaking. "But Sheila's pregnant now. I can't leave her." Too stunned to move, the hair on her thighs drying stiffly, she had stared at him leaving.

And Eric. Over and over, Eric. "We've had fun, Laura, but this is a *job*. My future. Don't get emotional over this, okay? It was fun."

Harder to make these ghosts hurt than the happy ones. She wants the beautiful ghosts, for all she knows about them. These betrayers are strangers, strangers. She stares and stares at them.

The same feeling she's ever had on betrayal: numb. Just numb.

She doesn't miss the men who left. She misses ones she loves, and hates: the lovers who once stayed. If only they would go away now. Go away, leave her in peace.

The pain stays.

She thinks about what Eric said about beating him to the other side. She goes out the next Saturday, buys a tiny gun from a local pawn shop and contemplates it for a long hour, Frank sleeping at her elbow where the bed used to be two years ago. Contemplates it until the plastic pearl handle sticks warmly to her fingers. But death is a land of ghosts, and how is someone who can't manage the ghosts of life to manage all the ghosts of death?

Or maybe she's just a coward.

Unable to point it at her own head, she turns it on sleeping Frank. "Bang," she says. Frank snores softly.

She crosses the room to where Donald is destroying the Venetian blind, futilely trying to rehang it. Aims. "Bang." The blind crashes to the floor and Donald, laughing, scoops it up. She walks into the living room and aims at the red overchair.

Eric isn't there.

Laura drops the gun. Somehow, it doesn't go off.

Somehow, Eric isn't there.

She approaches the chair slowly, afraid of things she can't guess at.

Just a chair. Empty.

She runs into the dining room, too fast to follow the side-to-side pattern, flashing past two Donalds and a Frank. Reaches the dining-room table.

Empty.

The back bedroom. The guest bed only ever shared with one person.

Empty.

The sink, where Donald or Frank never did dishes.

Empty.

Panicking, she runs outside to the front stoop. No roses wait for her there.

Back to the chair. She rips off the cushion, looking for she doesn't know what. Shakes the empty chair. Shakes it shakes it shakes it. Wrenches the chair back and forth with hysteric echoing clatters.

The phone rings. Laura jumps as though the gun were firing. She grips one velvet chair arm with each hand, presses her forehead into the back of the chair, breathes deeply. The phone keeps ringing. Trembling, she picks up the receiver.

"Ms. Hampton?" asks a strange voice. Not Eric. Not Eric.

"Yes?" Her voice is a squeak. She tries again. "Yes."

"I'm sorry to bother you. My name's Bill Chang. You don't know me. I was Eric Kennelly's roommate."

"Yes?"

"Um, well, your name is on this list he wanted me to call when—

Ms. Hampton, I'm calling to tell you he passed away this afternoon."

"Yes."

"Um, I'm sorry to have to tell you this like this. I wish we could talk, but he's got all these cousins, and he really wanted me to make all these calls—"

"Yes."

"I know this is a terrible thing to hear from a stranger—"

"When did it happen?"

"What? Oh, I'm sorry. Less than an hour ago. I just talked to his parents. Do you want to know when the funeral is?"

"No. Thank you, Mr. Chang. Goodbye."

She hangs up the phone. The red chair is a little out of place. She replaces the cushion and pushes the chair gently to its proper bit of wall. Sits in it. So comfortable. So empty.

The little pawnshop gun lies at her foot. She picks it up and wipes cold sweat from its handle. It really is a nice little gun; it fits sweetly in her hand.

Sitting in the empty red chair with the sweet little gun feels better than she's felt in a year. Longer. She shuts her eyes and luxuriates in the wonder of having a third of her home back to herself. No more paper plates—she can use the sink. She can eat at the table. She can sleep on the guest bed. Reborn possibilities warm her, spread from her heart to tingle in every limb, flow through her hand to warm the sweet little gun.

Later she picks up the phone and dials a memorized number she's never phoned before.

"Mrs. Prescott?" she says pleasantly. "Hi. You don't know me. I'm an old friend of your husband Frank's. Could you tell him I've run into a few old things of his around my place I'd like him to come pick up?—Whenever's convenient. Thanks so much."

She stretches back in the red overchair, listening to Mrs. Prescott telling her when Frank can come over, right hand wrapped comfortably around warm plastic grip.

"Yes, that'll be a big help." Laura smiles. "I'm just trying to clear out the house."

Things Not Seen

Her screen was slightly unbalanced toward green. It dulled reds, making it appear Dr. Herrera's face was streaked with chocolate syrup. Ginnie Erickson glanced at the security robot, which squatted near her hip, cabled into her workstation. "Hold it, please." The image froze. She hit a few keystrokes, until the blood was vivid red. "Take it at half speed." Herrera's head moved forward a bit, as though he were trying to peer through his gouged eyes, and he began to slump in his chair. "Quarter speed."

The viewpoint shifted crazily until Ralph Herrera filled the screen. Diagnostics–blood pressure, pulse–scrolled under the image of the dying scientist, measurements taken by the robot as it made itself into a temporary heart-lung machine, hooked to Herrera's circulatory system and oxygenating his blood.

Too late. His brain was scrambled by the icepick that had stabbed through his eyes. The security robot was not equipped with an EEG, or it could have registered its charge's brain-death and saved itself some trouble.

"Stop," Ginnie said. There was nothing striking left in the robot's memory until ten minutes later, when Drobisch, the security chief, arrived. She might have continued in fast scan, but Drobisch was standing behind her. She'd seen that part already. The digital recording would show his hasty arrival, shirttail untucked, gun in hand. He would bend over the corpse and say, "Shit. Damn it, Herrera, if you've cost me my job–" It did not seem politic to play forward to that point.

"So what's wrong with the stupid machine?" Drobisch asked.

"I don't know. Give me some time."

"Time? Time?" She suspected he was related to someone, somewhere. Surely there was no other reason a twit like him could hold his job.

"It's a very complicated stupid machine." She turned to the robot. "You're a complicated machine, aren't you?"

"Yes," said the robot, its pleasant voice coming from a speaker in its chest. She'd known the guy who recorded its core model vocabulary. He said it had taken a week, but the results were worth it, easy enough on the ears that she'd dated the voice's original for two months. She was only slightly miffed that in her six years of working with robots, no one had ever suggested her voice would make a good model.

"So simplify it," said Drobisch. "The stupid thing says Herrera came in, sat down, and suddenly had blood and eyeballs all over himself. It's a stupid waste of money. And it's useless to the company until we figure out what's wrong with it."

"The back of my neck is warm enough, though, thanks," she said. Drobisch stared at her. "Could you stop breathing down it for a while? You're making me itch."

"I think I'll watch."

"Then could you tell me why the company is into investigating this thing? Why don't you leave it to the cops?"

"It's company business."

"What in the world was he working on? Why did he even need a guard robot?"

"Forget that, missy. It's classified."

"It might help me know who was after him."

"That's none of your business. Your business is to figure out what's wrong with the stupid robot. Period. So do it."

Finally she ran the robot's memory forward through its entire futile attempt to keep Herrera alive. Drobisch squirmed and left before the playback reached his arrival at the scene. Ginnie had the little office back to herself.

She stretched, sighed, and told the robot, "Let's take it from the top. Eleven p.m., Friday night."

Four hours later she hadn't gotten anywhere. Interrogating the robot and examining its visual memory gave her the same result: a headache. She leaned on the desk, flexing her tired wrists.

"When did the last person leave the lab besides Herrera?"

"Eight forty-six p.m., seventeen seconds," said the robot.

"That was Jane Yonamura?"

"Yes."

"No one besides Dr. Herrera was in the lab between then and when Drobisch arrived at eleven twenty-six?"

"That is correct."

"Did Herrera look nervous?"

"Please contextually define 'nervous.'"

"Did he do anything unusual during that period?"

"He died."

Ginnie smiled. Literal-minded program. Others might anthropomorphize the robot, despite its resemblance to a large garbage can bristling with mechanical limbs and extrusions. She knew it was a sophisticated computer program housed in a wheeled mechanism. Real artificial intelligence was still down the road.

"Did he do anything unusual during the last period he was alone, before he died?"

"He spent 87% of that period at his computer terminal. He spent 9% of that period pacing. He spent 4% of that period in the bathroom. These percentages are in the normal range for Dr. Herrera's late-night activities since I was assigned to guard him."

"Why were you assigned to guard him?"

"That information is classified."

"What was he working on?"

"That information is classified."

Ginnie shook her head and looked at her notes. *Yonamura leaves, 8:46:17 p.m. Herrera goes to john, 11:08:51. H. back, 11:15:02. H. dead, 11:15:43. Drobisch arrives, 11:26:25.* It was odd that Herrera was murdered right after he got back from the bathroom, but that didn't help. Did someone sneak into the lab during the six minutes scientist and robot were away? Possible, but it didn't explain how the robot didn't see that person murder the scientist in plain sight.

Another thing she couldn't understand was how Herrera could sit still while someone jabbed an icepick through his eyes. She flinched just thinking about it. If he'd been drugged–but she'd been told blood workups hadn't found anything.

The robot had been instructed to tell her nothing that would reveal the nature of Herrera's work, but he had done nothing confidential in the hour and a half after his assistant left: there were no holes in what it told her. The robot's memory could be edited by a programmer, but any such edit would be recorded in deeply encrypted codes. She'd checked them. Its memories had not been touched in more than two months.

Her eyes stung. Either she was feeling sympathetic pains, or she'd been working too long.

"Off," she told the robot. She left it cabled into her computer so she could start again first thing in the morning.

George looked up from her book when Ginnie let herself in. "Long day," she commented. Ginnie grunted at her twin sister, the one named after their mother's native state. Their father was from Virginia: the family joke was that Ginnie—Virginia—was Daddy's girl, and Georgia was their mother's favorite. It was a durable enough joke that Ginnie worked with computers, like her father, and George did medical research, like her mother.

The other family joke was how lucky they were no one was from New Jersey.

"You're telling me." Ginnie hung her jacket on her side of the closet. "Hey, this is your umbrella. Keep it on your side!"

"Picky, picky. Fabulous mood you're in tonight." George was her double, wide-hipped, narrow-waisted, with too much dark curly hair to keep under perfect control. Every time Ginnie looked at her, she wanted to brush her own hair.

"You ever have some jerk leaning on you about some impossible task, and you'll be allowed to comment."

George grinned. She worked at their mother's lab, so she was always expected to put in late hours. But they'd recently finished a major project and were taking some time off. "What's up?"

"Get this. You know the guy who got killed the other day? The security robot completely flaked, didn't record the murder. I'm supposed to figure out what went wrong with it."

"Oh, now, that's interesting. Think you'll find out who killed him?"

Ginnie walked past her sister into the kitchenette. "That's 'none of my business.' I'm just supposed to find why the security robot screwed up." She took down a bowl and a box of raisin bran.

"Robots and computers. Very dull. The murder of Ralph Herrera, that's interesting. Hey, he's a fellow Caltech alum. You should catch his murderer to avenge the glory of our alma mater. And that's not a real dinner, you know."

Ginnie put the milk back in the refrigerator. "Tough. You cook a real dinner, I'll be glad to eat it."

"You order out for a real dinner, I'll be glad to warm it up in the microwave. So, the murder. Who offed him?"

"I don't know. Everything's very hush-hush. Drobish—he's the security idiot, he's got to really be sweating his job—won't tell me why. Maybe he's not in on it either, I don't know. I don't know Herrera's work, I don't know his social life, I don't know if he had negatives of Drobisch in bed with his German shepherd. I just have to find the bug." She took a big spoonful of cereal. "Of course, the idea that they spent so much money for a security droid that can't even spot a murderer is probably reason enough. But then, they're hiding the robot from the cops."

"I hate it when you talk with your mouth full. That's what I'd sound like, if I didn't have any manners. It's not a pretty thought, you know."

Ginnie crunched her cereal.

"Means, motive, opportunity," George said. Ginnie noticed belatedly that the novel George was reading was a Nero Wolfe. "You must know something we can deduce from."

"Opportunity, I don't understand. Motive, I haven't a clue. Means, an icepick right into the brains and swirled around a bit."

"Ugh. Can the icepick be traced?"

"That's something for the cops to do. I doubt it, though. I got a pretty good look at it in the robot's visual memory. It was an ordinary Sears icepick."

"Fingerprints?"

"Smudged palmprints, from what I hear."

"Could be his, if he tried to pull it out. What makes you think the robot didn't do it? Aren't you worried to be around the thing?"

Ginnie shook her head. "I made sure to ask about that. There was brain matter on the icepick. It would have got on the murderer's hands. There was none on the grasping limbs the robot could have used to hold the weapon, only blood and vitreous goop from the eyes. Anyway, the angle of entry was all wrong for a killer as short as the robot. Just right for a human murderer."

George marked her place in the Nero Wolfe and put it aside. "You're not bright enough to figure out the opportunity, and the means are mundane, if ugly. We'll have to work on motive."

Ginnie poured more cereal in her bowl. "I don't have to come home for this abuse, you know. I can go back to work and get it from Drobisch."

"I'm better at it, though."

"Only because you have more practice, and perfect genes."

"Motive, motive. Did you know this guy at all from work?"

"No. He's just one of those people who comes in, works constantly, and goes home. He didn't exactly hang out chatting in the cafeteria. He was working on something classified, they say."

"So it could be industrial sabotage." George frowned. "But why would a saboteur kill him in such a nasty way? Stabbing out his eyes. That seems so personal. Maybe symbolic. Like, oh, jealousy: 'You'll never look at another woman again!'"

"He doesn't sound like the ladykiller type," Ginnie said.

"That doesn't mean it couldn't have gone the other way around, right?"

"He's the kind of guy who spent all his time in the lab."

"So he was fooling around with someone in the lab, then. Was he married?" Ginnie shook her head. "So he's seeing someone at the lab, and she gets jealous. Maybe he isn't even fooling around on her. Maybe she's one of those crazed researchers who goes nuts after too much sleep deprivation."

"Maybe *you* are," Ginnie commented.

"Who's the last person who saw him alive?"

"His assistant, Jane Yonamura."

"Ah-hah!"

"Oh, come on, she doesn't look the type."

"They never do," George said wisely. "What's her line of work?"

"That one I do know. Before she was assigned to Herrera, she ran the clone lab we use." Ginnie helped design roboticized diagnostic stations, translating BioInnovation's doctors' expertise into programs that could detect increasingly fine signs of medical disorder. They went through scores of identical rabbits, mice and monkeys, testing the devices. Until she'd been tabbed to find a bug in a robot she'd had no hand in programming, the most frustrating part of Ginnie's job had been waiting the months it could take for a mouse genetically predisposed to a heart disorder to mature into symptoms for her programs to find.

"Tell you what," George said. "Herrera went to Tech years before us, but I'll bet I know some people from there who knew him. I'll call around and get the scoop on him for you. You should talk to Yonamura. Either she's the murderer, or she knows the other woman who's the murderer, or if something on their project got him killed, she may know about that, too."

"Drobisch will never let her talk. And solving murders isn't my job."

"You're a spoilsport. I'm going to call around anyway."

Ginnie went to get more milk.

She threw the printouts aside. "Gah!"

"I beg your pardon?" said the robot.

"It was, um, an interjection," Ginnie said. "It wasn't directed at you. It was directed at this damn documentation."

The robot was silent. It knew it did not have to answer a comment made to damn documentation, she thought.

Or to a lack of damn documentation. BioInnovations had only been able to obtain the non-proprietary parts of the robot's software from its designers, since for whatever reason they didn't want it known the robot had failed to prevent a murder. Ginnie had called the guy she'd dated, the one with the voice, but he had only worked on the robot's speech software. He was no help.

The software documentation the other company had supplied was terrible. She didn't think it had been tampered with to help preserve trade secrets. She'd written too much overhasty documentation herself.

She was looking in particular for a programming kludge that might have been written in to fix a bug the earlier programmers couldn't find, what she called the Use a Bigger Hammer school of programming. She'd done it herself, though never as sleazily as the programmer who, faced with a program that unaccountably would sometimes add two and two to make five, inserted code that said, *If 2 + 2 = 5, then 5 = 4.*

Anything that obvious would leap out at her, but it wasn't likely to be that obvious.

She also had to look for sabotage. So far the robot appeared to work the way it was supposed to, with no signs of tampering.

If she were actually working on solving the murder, rather than trying to find an invisible bug in a Byzantine robot, that could be interesting.

She leaned back in her desk chair. It creaked. "I've been listening to George too much." The robot swiveled to focus its attention on her. "I'm going to check on something," she told it. "Don't go anywhere."

"Noted," said the robot.

"Not possible," Drobisch said. His desk was enormous, a monster of dark-stained wood and iron trim.

"She was the last living person to see the robot working. She might have noticed something that would help me."

"She didn't."

"You're not the computer expert. Let me talk to her."

"We're concerned about her safety."

So you do think Herrera got killed because of what he was working on, she thought. "Look, I just want to ask her questions about the robot's functioning. Something that might look like nothing to you, and to her, might be the clue I need."

Drobisch glowered at her.

She rose to go. "Okay. Maybe I can find this glitch anyway. It probably doesn't matter. The cops will probably figure out that portable heart-lung machine you hooked to Herrera was the second one. If they guess there was a robot at the scene, they'll impound it, and it won't be my headache."

"Wait," Drobisch said. Her hand was on the doorknob. She turned. "You can talk to her. At lunch, tomorrow."

As she'd figured. If she found the bug before the cops knew about the robot, they could erase all its memory and know they could safely use it again when it was finally returned by the cops. "Thanks."

"I'll be sitting in. Maybe I can help you." The sullen tone of his voice was a warning.

Jane Yonamura was a thin woman, older than Ginnie, though it was hard to judge: maybe thirty, maybe thirty-five. She sat across from Ginnie at the cafeteria table, not meeting her eyes. Ginnie remembered that was a characteristic of Japanese politeness. Otherwise Yonamura seemed American enough.

"I'm sorry about Dr. Herrera," Ginnie said. "Had you known him long?" Drobisch shifted in the chair beside her. You can damn well put up with politenesses, she thought. Anyone would ask that.

"We worked together for two years," Yonamura said. "I knew him as well as you know most people you work with. It's difficult to get used to his absence."

"I'm very sorry," Ginnie said.

Drobisch cleared his throat. Yonamura was silent.

"Did you notice anything unusual about the robot that night?"

"I really couldn't say, Ms. Erickson. I'm not an expert on such things. Dr. Herrera understood computers, but he was a very clever man. I'm an ordinary cellular biology expert; I only deal with computers and robots to the extent I need to for my work."

"That's what my sister always says, that she hates dealing with computers." Drobisch ostentatiously looked at his watch. "But she uses them more than she thinks about. I'm sure you noticed something."

"I can't think of anything."

"Well, you were working late."

"We usually did."

Just working? Ginnie wondered. Probably. They had a robot watching them for the last several weeks. "Did you have the robot assist you in any way?" The robot had been instructed not to reveal anything about Herrera and Yonamura's work to her.

"No. Well, Dr. Herrera may have asked it to time some processes, or hold an instrument. Only very simple things."

"That's good. Did it have trouble understanding any of his instructions that night?"

"No. Let me think about that. —No, I really don't think so. As I said, he never asked it to do very much. I'm not even certain he talked to it that night."

Now, you'd remember what Herrera did the night he was murdered, Ginnie thought. It was only five days ago, and it had been a memorable night. "It'd be a waste to have such a state-of-the-art robot around and not have it do anything to help out, wouldn't it? I mean, I wonder what the accountants thought about okaying such an expensive piece of machinery. I guess you guys were doing something important."

"I suppose someone thought so," said Yonamura, impassively. Ginnie could hear Drobisch breathing. The man breathed loud. He must have practiced being noticeable.

"Did either of you talk to the robot? Did it say anything?"

"It might have. I don't recall."

"I was going to ask if it was showing any difficulties with language, or if it stuttered, or repeated itself. You don't remember if it spoke?"

"I don't," Yonamura said.

"What about its movements? Did it seem to have any trouble navigating?"

"Not to the best of my memory. It isn't something I'd have paid attention to."

"You're not getting anywhere here, Erickson," Drobisch said. "We all have work to do."

No kidding, I'm not, Ginnie thought. Yonamura was polite, but opaque: deliberately so, she was sure. That might have to do with Drobisch's presence. Perhaps.

"Thank you anyway," she told Yonamura, who smiled slightly and accepted Ginnie's handshake.

"It's driving me crazy," she told her sister. "Three days of this, and the robot makes no more sense than ever. No—the robot makes as *much* sense as ever. And it's probably got a hundred man-years of software in it. I could be looking forever." She rubbed her face, yawning. "If only they weren't too paranoid to bring in a team of people to look over the thing. The best way to spot a bug is to bring in a new perspective, but I can tell Drobisch doesn't even like having one person look at it."

"You saw Yonamura?" George asked.

"Oh, yeah. Speaking of brick walls. That woman's not going to talk about anything."

"Buried passions?"

"Buried everything. I can't guess what kind of secrets she's keeping. Maybe she just has more respect for non-disclosure agreements than I do."

"Hey, if you can't tell someone who shares your genetic material, who can you tell?" George said. "I'll never tell. Let them think I'm you."

"You wouldn't pass the retina ID check they made me take when I signed all those forms."

"So I won't let them stare deeply into my eyes. They'd never check. Even if they thought about you having a twin, the world's full of idiots who think twins have the same fingerprints and retina prints." As teenagers, George and Ginnie had read too much science fiction about clones, who were nothing but high-tech twins, not only having the same fingerprints, but lockstep personalities. They hated that. "Here's your surprise bonus today for having a nosey twin." George tossed a bound document on the kitchen table.

"What's this?"

"I drove over to Tech today to see if anyone had any old gossip about Herrera. Nothing. He had a girlfriend junior year from City College, but it didn't last." Ginnie snorted. She'd never thought much of guys who had to leave campus to get girlfriends. "So I looked up his doctoral dissertation, just so it wouldn't be a complete waste of time driving to Pasadena."

"It's always a waste of time driving to Pasadena," Ginnie said automatically, picking up the binder. "'Induced Heuristics and Rote Learning in Mammals?' Sounds like a page-turner."

"I still say Yonamura did him in, but if they weren't hot and heavy, and it was sabotage, this could be a clue to whatever they were working on."

"It was twelve years ago," Ginnie said. "It could have nothing at all to do with whatever he was doing for the company." She flipped through the pages. "And it's really badly written. Do they make you write dissertations this way? Thank god I didn't go for a doctorate."

"I had a look at it," George said. "There's some theoretical stuff about ways to treat people who've lost abilities due to strokes or other brain trauma."

"Like icepicks?"

"Ick. Like, say, someone has a microstroke, and can't tie his shoelaces anymore. Herrera thinks it should be possible to zap the whole subroutine for tying shoelaces into a brain."

"How?"

"I'm going to reread it. It's pretty thick going, and I never read much neurology. Most of this paper is about white rats and bunny rabbits. He only mentions people toward the end."

"That's the interesting part, though, isn't it?" Ginnie said. She squinted at a thicket of graphs relating in some way to brain chemicals she'd never heard of. "Programming human brains. Just think how a military organization would slaver over that."

"I have," George said. "So industrial sabotage goes back on the motive list. And so does international intrigue."

"Oh, great," said Ginnie. "Now I prefer the theory about a sex-crazed research assistant stabbing his eyes out."

"Either way, poor sap. Wonder if he saw it coming."

"It could explain why Yonamura is so quiet. This might be dangerous business to know anything about."

"If it's related to what Herrera was working on for BioInnovations," said George.

"I'm going to ask around some more. Maybe he told someone what he was working on."

"Listen," Ginnie said. She knew she couldn't stop her sister from working a puzzle through to its finish. She was intrigued herself, but she was also feeling queasy. She reached across the table and took her twin's hand. "Be careful."

George smiled and squeezed her fingers.

She was running the robot's memory through the last ten minutes before Herrera's death. The picture jiggled as the robot trundled through the hallway behind the scientist. Herrera went into the end stall of the men's room; the robot focused on the door. Someone had taped an old Gary Larson cartoon to it, so yellowed it was brown: it showed a laboratory filled with dead cats in lab coats. Curiosity, it seemed, had killed them.

Herrera came out of the stall and walked briskly out of the bathroom. He did not stop to wash his hands. Ginnie shook her head. The robot had to hurry to keep up. He stopped at the lab door, and the robot preceded him into the room and took up its customary position in the corner opposite the door, from which it could see everything. Herrera walked into the room and sat at his terminal. She isolated the keyboard in closeup. The keys Herrera hit were *A, 6, Caps Lock, Shift, J, Y, Delete, G, H, 2, Tab*. The sequence looked nonsensical. She frowned.

That was the point the door suddenly slammed shut; the robot glanced at the source of the sound, only for an instant.

Gore was running from Herrera's eyes when it glanced back.

Someone cleared his throat behind her. "You have two days."

"Two days until what?"

"I've spoken to your department," Drobisch said. Your supervisor agrees they're overextended in salary base. He may not be able to keep you on."

"Wait a minute."

"I've told him, of course, that since you've been on loan to the security department, we'd like to help. We might be able to squeeze out some money to move into their budget. Out of gratitude. If we were grateful."

This was nearly a subtle move. She should be impressed. "Come on. We're not talking about a payroll program. There are reams of code in this robot. You can't expect one programmer to find a bug in a week!"

"There are a lot of programmers. BioInnovations can't be expected to employ them all." Drobisch looked smug. He turned on his heel and left.

"Damn it!"

He was setting her up to be the fall guy. Not his fault the security robot didn't work: the company employed idiot programmers who couldn't work the thing. No matter she'd hardly seen the robot before the murder. She suspected Drobisch was in a position to alter her employment records.

He was right about one thing. Southern California, which ten years ago had looked like a bottomless pool of employment for good programmers, was finally saturated with them. And even when you lived with your sister, rents were outrageous. It took both of them to afford a two-bedroom place. The cost of water alone could break her, if she went long without a job.

She might even have to move to New Jersey.

"Damn it."

"We're not going to talk about me finding a new roommate," George said firmly. "We're going to solve this mystery."

Ginnie was lying on the sofa, her arms wrapped around a cushion, thinking. "If I have to move out, Mom will want you to move back with her."

"Not a chance. I love Mom and all, but give me a break. It's nice not to have talked to her for a week, for a change."

"You haven't told her? Good. She'd just worry. Did you find out anything about Yonamura?"

"No." George bit her lip. "I'm afraid I sort of wasted today. I wish I'd known Drobisch was going to lean on you."

"Well, you didn't know."

"Yeah, but if you lose your job— I was talking to some Lloydies about Herrera, back when he lived there. You know he lived in Lloyd House, just like I did?"

"No. Small world." Ginnie had an old college friend who'd dropped out of physics and started a small import business up in Oregon. Maybe he could use a programmer to make the shipping end of it more efficient. If she could get used to living with pine trees. Or maybe she could get a job on the loading dock. She hugged the cushion to her cheek.

"They were telling me stories about his Ditch Day stack. It was pretty memorable."

On Senior Ditch Day at Caltech, the seniors set puzzles, called "stacks," for the underclassmen to solve. The underclassmen had to solve the puzzle to gain entry to the senior's room. If they didn't find a "bribe"—usually junk food—waiting for them there, they had the right to counterstack the senior's room, giving her a taste of her own medicine.

Ginnie, distracted by killer finals, had simply thrown together a quiz for her stack. When the group trying to get into her room answered some trivia questions on her computer and solved what she'd thought was a fairly knotty programming puzzle, the computer told them where they could find her room key. She'd left a keg of beer and ten pounds of chocolate in the room, and when she got back from her Ditch Day trip to Disneyland, she found nothing but candy wrappers remaining of the bribe.

She still regretted not taking the time to come up with a finesse stack, something the underclassmen would bash their brains against all day but which would be obvious, in light of the clues, when they found out what it was.

"They got to his room and found a video monitor and a joystick outside the door," George said. "And a note that just said, 'Get the key or solve why it can't be done.'"

"Sounds like a good one," Ginnie said, interested despite herself.

"When they turned on the video monitor, it showed the interior of his room, like the camera was next to the door. It looked ordinary enough, but the floor was entirely cleared, and in the middle of it was the room key, and this little cart, with an arm in front and an antenna sticking up."

"The joystick."

"Yeah, one of them picked up the joystick and moved it around, and the cart turned around with it. One button on the joystick raised and lowered the arm, and the other made the cart go forward or backward. The arm had a magnet on it, and there was a washer taped to the key, so the magnet could pick it up."

"Too easy. There's a catch."

"You bet. It looked like the idea was to maneuver the cart over to the door with the key, and get it to push it out under the door. But they couldn't quite get the cart to work right. It'd start toward the door, and suddenly veer off in the wrong direction. Or it would stop moving. Or the key would fall off."

"Some kind of kink programmed into the cart's movement."

"They thought of that. They plotted all the unexplained movements and looked for a pattern. Like, if you turn it 180 degrees to the left, maybe it would go backward. Well, it did sometimes, and it didn't sometimes."

"So it had random error programmed into it, and that's why they couldn't get it to work?"

"But how do you 'prove' that? It's a finesse stack: there has to be something big and deceptively obvious they can point to, or Herrera's screwed it up. They're starting to get very annoyed, because they can see the room and there's no bribe they can see in it. These are students who are seriously looking forward to skipping the counterstack and just trashing his room if they solve the stack. It looks like he expected it to be impossible to solve, and that's not fair."

"What did it turn out to be?" Ginnie asked.

"Think about it. There are three components of the puzzle they can look at: there's the remote-controlled cart, and the joystick, and the video monitor/camera setup. They can't get to the cart, except by experimenting with the joystick and watching on the monitor."

"The joystick."

"They took it apart, carefully, and looked at it. Nothing funny in the joystick that they could see."

"The monitor?"

"It was late in the day when this one bright freshman began to wonder if the monitor was showing them the whole story. Some big-shot junior guy had the joystick, but she finally talked him into handing it to her. She moved the cart all the way to the back wall, and started to make it go back and forth, against the wall, as fast as she could."

"What did that prove?"

"In the middle of the room, the cart blinked out of existence on the video monitor. She moved it back, and half of it was gone. Then it came back again."

"You've lost me."

"Remember when we were kids watching a weather report, and the reporter was wearing a green tie, and you could see Indiana right through it?"

"I—oh! It was a chroma key setup!"

"She pounded on the door and shouted 'Open up, Ralph!', and Herrera opened the door from the inside. The whole back wall of the room was draped in green, he'd painted the floor green, and he was wearing a green bodysuit and a green hood."

"He'd been in the room all along."

"Yep. She'd proved why they couldn't get the key. It was one of those old-fashioned setups that screened out greens, the kind they used when they wanted it to look like the weather guy was standing in front of a weather map or a live shot of a sunset or something."

"I suppose he could find all the equipment for that on campus," Ginnie said.

"Actually, I think he salvaged it from a station that was upgrading its technology. Just like on the weather report, where the camera saw green, the chroma key showed a video image he'd taken earlier instead, of the normal back and floor of the room. So in his green coverup, he was invisible to the camera. As long as he stayed behind the cart, from camera view, he could mess with its movements without being detected."

"Not bad."

"There's this big lump covered with green cloth in the back of the room, and he rips it off: champagne on ice, this big pastry spread, the works. He sort of cheated by not having actually ditched on Ditch Day, but he sounds like an okay guy. It's too bad he's dead." George sighed. "He had chocolate eclairs for them. I never solved a stack that got me chocolate eclairs."

"Huh." Ginnie sat up and put the cushion down. "So there was one other factor in his stack puzzle, besides the cart, and the joystick, and the camera and monitor."

"Which is?"

"Him. Herrera."

"Good morning, Erickson," Drobisch said.

"Morning," she said, smiling.

She seemed awfully confident for someone who would be canned in eight hours, he thought. She wasn't bad-looking, but she had an attitude problem. "This is your last day, you know."

She smiled again and walked the other way down the hall. He put her out of his mind.

"Good morning, Mr. Drobisch."

"Morning," he grunted. He was almost at his office when he turned around. Who was that? Red suit jacket, blue jeans, brown hair. Erickson? Hadn't he already seen her?

Drobisch hated déjà vu in the morning. He decided he needed another cup of coffee. Yonamura could not be allowed to talk to anyone. He'd spend today making sure she knew that. It was an aggravation: no wonder he was distracted.

"This is to distract it." Ginnie held up the sound synthesizer. "It has about twenty seconds of silence programmed in before it shouts bloody murder. So timing's important on this experiment."

"Got it," George said. "You want me to walk over and sit in this chair? That's it?"

"That's it. Do it as smoothly as you can. Take even steps."

"Okay. Ready when you say."

"Now," said Ginnie. The robot was cabled to her workstation, on idle. She toggled it on with the joystick she'd rigged.

George walked across the room. The robot watched. She sat.

Ginnie waited a beat. Then she walked across the room, toward George. As she neared her twin, the sound synthesizer cried "Help! Burglar! Murder! Stop!" The robot swiveled toward the alarm. Ginnie toggled it back to idle.

"Let's see what we've got," she said. "You wait outside. I don't want it to see you again."

She turned the robot on again. "When did you last see me?" she asked.

"At 9:09 this morning."

"What did I do?"

"You entered this room. You walked to the northeast corner and sat down."

"How many times did I cross the room to the northeast corner this morning?"

"Once."

"Once?"

"Correct."

"Do you know what you've got, robot? You've got some let-five-equal-four code. You've got a kludge, and I know who else knew that.

Maybe two people who knew that."

"Do you require a response from me?"

"No, thanks. I've already got everything from you that I need." She turned the robot back to idle and hit the codes on her keyboard that would allow her to erase its memory of the morning's experiment. They could find traces of the editing, but maybe they wouldn't bother. With any luck, the robot would be on the scrapheap tomorrow.

"You can come back in."

"Good," said George. She shut the door behind her. "All your coworkers are staring at me. I think they're wondering why you're spending your morning standing outside your office. Did you get what you needed?"

"Yes," said Ginnie. "I'm almost certain what happened. I just need to pry Drobisch loose from Yonamura long enough to talk to her."

"Oh, that sounds like fun. Remember third grade, when we'd confuse Ms. Jefferson who was who?" George picked up Ginnie's extension. "Drobisch, please." Pause. "He's not in his office? You'd better page him and tell him to come see Virginia Erickson right now. No, this will not wait. Now!" She slammed the receiver down.

"How will you hold him?"

"I'll threaten a civil suit for wrongful termination of employment. I can doubletalk on that for at least half an hour."

"I owe you several."

"Nineteen, now. But who's keeping track?"

Yonamura was peering into a microscope and did not look up. "Mr. Drobisch, we've nothing to talk about. I've told you everything I know."

"I don't need you to tell me everything, Dr. Yonamura."

"Ms. Erickson?" Yonamura pushed her hair back. "I don't think it's a good idea for you to be here."

"Is it bugged?"

"Bugged? Oh, you mean a microphone. No, I don't–I don't think so. I think I found it." She avoided Ginnie's eye, as she had the first time they met. "I really have nothing to tell you about your robot."

"I want to mention a couple of things to you. I want to know if I'm understanding things right. If I do, you have nothing to worry about from me."

Yonamura was silent, watching her.

"I've seen Dr. Herrera's dissertation. It was about an idea called 'induced heuristics.' I don't know what you brought to the project, but I want to guess. I want to guess you can force-grow clones to early maturity."

"I don't know why you think so."

"You might want to know that I've discovered a bug in the robot after all. Actually, I've discovered the programming fix that covers up a bug."

Yonamura folded her hands in her lap and waited.

"I think when they were designing the robot, it had a glitch that made it think it had seen the same thing more than once. A sort of robot déjà vu. If you rolled a ball in front of it, it might think it saw that ball roll by twice, or, worst case, it might get stuck in a loop and see nothing but that ball roll by, an infinite number of times. That would be a problem."

"I suppose it would. It's not my specialty."

"Dr. Herrera understood computers, though. And perception, and behavior. He needed all of that for the work you were doing, didn't he? You grow the clones, he works on their brains."

"Dr. Herrera's work was classified. And difficult. Even if I were at liberty to explain it to you, I wouldn't be able to."

"That's okay. I'll make a crude guess. Herrera was inventing a way to put behaviors into empty brains. Like the brains of force-grown clones. It's the only thing I can think of that explains why Herrera's still alive. Are you in contact with him? Do you know where he is?"

Yonamura leapt to her feet. "Ms. Erickson! Dr. Herrera is dead! How can you say–"

"Settle down! I'm just babbling nonsense. Not even worth repeating outside this room. Just let me finish. If you two were working on a project to turn blank-minded clones into programmed zombies, and if he wanted out–if he didn't like what he thought was going to be done with it, but he was afraid BioInnovations or its clients would go after him if he ran–you could use the robot's little undocumented feature."

Ginnie licked her lips. Her mouth was dry. She'd tried not to think through the implications of her solution, but she couldn't avoid it now. Yonamura looked like she wanted to run.

Ginnie said, "Here's where I get really nonsensical: You've developed a way to force clones to rapid maturity. You've made a Herrera clone, all grown up but no mind to speak of. With his neurochemicals and electronics and whatever, Herrera gives it a simple program: stand on this toilet until tapped on the shoulder, leave the bathroom, walk down a hall, go into a room, sit in a chair, hit some random computer keys, wait.

"The real Herrera, dressed identically, follows immediately behind the clone, careful to walk the same way the clone was programmed to.

"Now, here's the beauty part: he knows, maybe from noticing the way it perceived little cloned, behavior-programmed bunnies, that the robot discounts anything it believes it's identically seen, immediately before. Completely discounts it. Doesn't perceive it. That's how its programmers kludged the déjà vu bug."

Yonamura sat, slowly.

"All he needs is to distract the robot long enough to stab into his clone's nearly blank brain, incidentally destroying the clone's unique retina patterns, in case anyone thought to check. If he ducks out of sight quickly enough, when the robot's first-aid functions take over, it won't have time to see him escape. While its kludge kept it from perceiving him come in."

"You can't prove any of this," Yonamura said quietly.

"They didn't put the robot on him to guard him from the competition, did they? That was a side-benefit, but they really wanted to make sure he didn't try anything funny. The robot was there to report if he did, and to intimidate him so he wouldn't try it in the first place."

"That's what we thought." Yonamura's tone was even.

Ginnie had to work to keep her own voice low. "Our advantage is that Drobisch wants to bury any evidence that might show Herrera's death was his fault. If you stay quiet, you may be okay."

"Dr. Herrera was the only person who fully understood his theories. I'm counting on them not watching me quite as closely. I'd planned to get away as soon as he had enough time to cover his tracks. We weren't counting on the fraud never being discovered. We only hoped, if they thought a competitor had killed him, that it would give him enough time."

"I hope it does. I don't want to know how much money is involved in this. I don't want to know which governments would pay for this technology. I do have one question."

"What?" asked Dr. Yonamura.

"Herrera's techniques—were they only useful on blank brains? Or could they be used on your brain, or mine?"

Yonamura looked Ginnie directly in the eye. She said nothing.

George was gone when Ginnie returned. It took less than half an hour to find the kludge in the robot's code, now that she knew what to look for. She made a simple deletion. Then she packed her personal effects.

"Erickson!" Drobisch thundered. He stormed through her doorway. "You are finished at this company. You are finished everywhere. Your work record shows inefficiencies that—"

"You're right, Mr. Drobisch," Ginnie said. She nodded at the security robot, which stared unmoving at the doorway, watching images of Drobisch storm in again, and again, and again. "I not only didn't find the glitch in the security robot, but the bug seems to have gotten worse. It's a mess."

"Goddamn stupid machine! I told them not to—"

"You were right. Under the circumstances, I think I should give my notice." She picked up her box of personal items and squeezed past him as he gaped.

Would Drobisch be more interested in burying anything that would make him look bad to his superiors than he was in following her? It was a fair bet.

Oregon or New Jersey? She wondered which one Herrera would choose.

The Story So Far

We grew up in the same small town, in the same short story.

A first glimpse of classroom. Blinds raised, a sunny day. Mrs. Zelinski appears, short, gray, plump, pulling down a map with a stick with a hook at the end. In another moment she is wearing a plaid cotton dress, and it is ugly.

I am sitting at a desk among two dozen other murky students, but I do not know who I am yet. I only know Mrs. Zelinski, talking about Argentina, which hooks down to a point at the bottom of the map, and Dennis.

Then Dennis looks across at Sylvia, and I see her for the first time. Sylvia happens before I do, but only by an instant, because Dennis sees me sitting on the other side of her, so that I am there when we first see that she is beautiful.

Sylvia is beautiful. She is beautiful in the way few people are in their first rush of adolescence, which explains to me for the first time that that is how old we are. In this way I learn: Mrs. Zelinski's dress, tan and gray plaid, hitched up on the right where it catches in the belt, is ugly. Sylvia's blonde hair pushed over to one side, Sylvia's skin so fair it glows, with no trace of the acne I know now I have, Sylvia's soft blue dress gliding down around her new breasts and her long legs crossed at the heels, under her chair—these are beautiful. There can be no doubt Dennis is struck with an awkward awe at the sight of her.

Dennis glances past her for a moment at me and I blush. I know he doesn't even see me (now I know my name is Emmy Cluff, and I am small and flat and forgettable) past the fleeting notice that I am a little pale mouse next to Sylvia. Still, Dennis has looked straight at me, and I blush and look down at the top of my desk. I do not care about Dennis, but I have to blush.

Mrs. Zelinski's stick crashes on her desk and Dennis is no longer looking at me. Now I don't have to look at my desk, so I look up, first to see Argentina, pale green on the map against the robin's-egg Atlantic Ocean. And then I look over at Sylvia.

She winks at me. Dennis is stammering at Mrs. Zelinski and doesn't see. Mrs. Zelinski says something and Dennis looks embarrassed. I am thinking, why do I have to have a dumb name like Emmy Cluff? I wish my name were Sylvia.

Mrs. Zelinski says something else, and that is the last I see of Mrs. Zelinski or the seventh-grade classroom.

It is a summer game of softball. I think more has happened between, but it is the next time I am in the story. I stand on the sidelines watching Dennis come to the plate. He is bigger now. While he hits his bat on the plate, I sneak a look down at myself. I am bigger too, but not much bigger in the place I am looking. I look around and see Sylvia, on the other sideline. She is wearing shorts that show how long and slim her legs are. I am in baggy blue jeans and a dull blue blouse.

There are other kids with names here, mostly on Dennis's team, but I can feel that they won't be very important to the story, and most of them don't even have names.

Dennis strikes out. He comes over to the side. Sylvia is laughing with another boy on the team. Dennis walks up to me.

"What are you doing Saturday?" It is the first time I really hear his voice, which is medium-deep and sounds like it's getting deeper. It is only the second scene that I have been alive.

"I have a clarinet lesson," I say. Do I play clarinet?

"No, I mean Saturday night," Dennis says.

I blush again, which is annoying. This story does not have much subtlety. "Nothing, I guess," I say.

Dennis glances over at Sylvia, who is laughing loudly enough to hear from here. If the look is meant to be surreptitious, it misses, so it probably isn't. "Want to go to a movie?"

I feel the blush burn harder. I want to shout Stop that! I say "Okay," which is all that's required of me, because there isn't a break, exactly, but the doorbell rings and I have parents, hovering over me in the front hall of our house.

My mother rushes to the front door and lets Dennis in. My dress is too tight in the ribcage and I guess too short, too. It shows I don't have many opportunities to dress up. As Dennis comes in I sneak a look at my parents. They are both short, plump, with brown hair the color of mine, my father's thinning and my mother's held round about her head with too much hair spray. They aren't much of a job of imagining parents.

As Dennis comes up to take my arm in an oddly courtly gesture, I wonder if he notices the gaps in the story, or if being the center of attention is enough to keep his mind occupied. I want to ask.

"Is the movie downtown okay?" he asks.

"Sure," I say. I walk to the door with him, feeling heavy. I must weigh twenty pounds more than I did in the first scene. My mother beams.

The movie playing is a second run of something. Of what, I'm not sure: I watch the screen but I see only random shapes, a shadow of something that is either a car chase or a dancing scene. Dennis cranes his neck over the balcony railing. I sit back, squinting my eyes against the darkness. I'm still taller than he is. I can see where he's looking: down in the main section, in front, over to the left. She is with the boy from the softball game, and she is pulling his head over to kiss him.

I shake my head in admiration. Right in front of the theater like that. Anyone else would hide in back, in the balcony. The longer I am alive, the more of the story's assumptions I understand. Now I know that Sylvia does not have a good reputation, and that Dennis doesn't dare talk to her. I wonder why this story seems to define girls by what boys think of them.

Then I realize the only reason the story has Sylvia kissing the other boy in plain sight is for what Dennis will think about that. I worry: Does she want to kiss the boy? Does she understand it's a show for Dennis? Does she enjoy it anyway?

I'm thinking about that when Dennis puts his hand up my blouse, and I push it away once and then do not. I am not thinking about his hand. It's the way the story goes, his hand groping randomly over me, and I can't do anything about it but think. I wonder what Sylvia thinks as she puts her tongue in the softball boy's mouth. I wonder if anyone thinks besides me. I hope Sylvia does.

Now it's a dance. Banners over the gym floor say JUNIOR PROM. I'm in a different dress, but it still feels tight. I glance down to see that I'm straining at the front of it. Must be a recent development, har har.

I am far from the center again, standing by the bleachers. It's more focused in the center of the gym, and it takes me no time to pick out Dennis, dancing with Sylvia. Her hair is longer and ripples like a waterfall when she moves. The story is dim where I am, and I find I can ripple my fingers in imitation of that watery shimmer, on purpose. I wonder if her hair feels like water. I run my fingers through my own hair.

Sylvia laughs. "What in the world are you doing?"

I drop my hands, startled. Dennis is still far away on the gym floor, arguing with some boys. Sylvia is grinning at me.

"Trying to make my hair like yours," I blurt.

The words come out exactly the way my thoughts are in my head. That's a surprise. I realize this isn't part of the story; the story continues with the boys slowly circling each other on the dance floor.

"It isn't, though," I say, a little more careful with these words, these words I am controlling myself. "It just hangs there." As long as Dennis doesn't see or hear us, I can really talk. "This is stupid, but— can I touch your hair?"

Sylvia looks slantwise at me. She doesn't say a word. I'm afraid she's really just a prop in the story after all, and I feel sadder than I'd learned how to feel before.

She takes my hand.

The argument across the gym is becoming more animated. I see one of the boys is the boy from the softball game and the movie. Sylvia's hand is warm and dry. Mine feels clammy. I am embarrassed, fascinated, as she raises my hand. I feel my pulse against the warmth of her skin.

The boy from the softball game is hitting Dennis in the face. The rest of the boys stand like statues.

Sylvia pulls my fingers through her hair. It is soft and smooth, but it isn't water and it isn't magic, it's hair, like mine. I like that.

I say, "I wish I could dance like you do."

"Oh, dancing," she says, dismissing it. "That's just for the story. What I do is think. You do that, too."

She smiles and I think she is going to touch my face when the boy from the softball game comes and takes her away, just like that. Dennis appears, a bruise around his mouth, his eye beginning to swell. "Let's leave," he says, and I realize I came to the dance with him. I want to wave goodbye to Sylvia, but my fingers cannot move that way when Dennis is looking at me. Instead they go up to touch his mouth, gently. He winces.

"I'm sorry," my voice says. "I should have told you Ralph was looking for you."

"It's a free country," he grumbles. "People can dance, can't they? Can't people do what they want?"

I don't know, I want to say. Can I?

"Of course," I say. "Could you take me home now? This is a stupid dance anyhow." He takes my hand to lead me from the gym. His fingers trap mine. They do not pulse with possibility. I look for Sylvia in the parking lot as we get into the car and the scene ends, but she is nowhere to be seen.

I am driving down the central part of town. I see Dennis and Sylvia walking along the sidewalk. Dennis seems to catch a glimpse of the car I am driving. He pulls Sylvia into an ice-cream shop. I want to try out how fast the car can drive on the expressway but

I am crying on the front steps of my parents' house. "The scholarship didn't come through," I say. "You know my parents can't afford to send me to the school you're going to." Tears feel weird. There is a teasing little breeze: it catches them in cold stripes down both sides of my face.

"I won't go. I'll take classes with you at the community college." Dennis has a brave look on his face, but his eyes look trapped. Does he want to stop the plot to see what happens, too? I want to ask him. I try. I open my mouth.

"Don't be stupid," I say. "You have to go. You'll learn all sorts of things. You'll be an engineer. And you'll meet lots of girls as beautiful as–prettier than me. You'll probably end up living in Paris or something, and I'll stay in the suburbs." I guess this is a fight. I don't like the way I fight. I don't seem to do it in a very straightforward manner.

"I won't," he says. "I'll come back."

"You won't," I say. If he doesn't, is the story over for me? I know this is Dennis's story, though I wish it were Sylvia's. But not mine. If the story's spotlight were on me all the time, I wouldn't have been able to say what I wanted to say to Sylvia in the gym. She liked that I thought my own thoughts.

"I will," he says. "I'll marry you, Emmy."

I cry harder, which seems pretty stupid. Then my face is dry and we're in a jewelry store and I say "It's the most beautiful ring I ever saw, Dennis!" He kisses me. I see Sylvia through the store window. She puckers up and squoonches her eyes shut, making fun of the way Dennis kisses. She winks at me and skips away.

Dennis didn't even see her.

That's interesting.

The long train of my dress catches and pulls on the red carpet. I am taller than my father now, walking beside me, but he doesn't look any different or more formed than he did last time.

"Dearly beloved," the minister says.

Dennis puts another ring on my finger. He kisses the bride.

I throw the bouquet at the reception. Sylvia catches it. I try to catch her eye but everything is moving too fast.

He is carrying me into a hotel room. I am in bed. My clothes are gone. He gets on top of me. His legs are heavy on mine and he smells of sweat. He murmurs unintelligibly.

The scene breaks.

Dennis comes home. He's been doing things, but I don't know what, and I can't ask. I'm just in the apartment, which isn't much different from my parents' house except it's smaller.

"How was your day?" I ask. I know the story's been moving since the wedding. I can feel it. I wish I knew if Sylvia is still part of it.

"Fine," Dennis says. Then he makes a smile and says "Fine, honey." And he puts his mouth on top of mine and bends me back. That's that.

"The doctor said there's no reason I shouldn't have children," I'm telling Dennis. "He said just relax."

"Do you ever relax?" Dennis mutters. How would I know?

I bring him a dinner I must have cooked. Pot roast. I put it in front of him and he doesn't say anything. He just eats it. I don't say anything either. I don't think I like being married. My scenes are shorter and there's less for me to look at. I wonder if things will change, or the story will just end, or my part in it will end. I wonder if I'll know it when my part in the story is over, or if I'll just stop.

"A person can see who he wants to see, can't he? It's a free country, isn't it?" Dennis is shouting at me.

This marriage must not be very pleasant.

Sylvia walks by the front window and waves at me. I'm surprised she's there, and I want to go see her. But Dennis is still shouting.

"Don't let me stop you," I say in a low mean voice. Why should I sound angry? What is Dennis to me? He has made me blush, and marry him, and he bent me back in bed, but that doesn't touch me. I just have to say the things I have to say. We have not been in groups of people, so I could think my thoughts in the background while he interacts with someone else, not since the wedding. It all moves too fast now. I have to try to figure things out in the little moments between shouting and tears.

"I won't!" Sylvia is back outside the window. She lifts her fingers and makes antennae behind the back of Dennis's head, where only I can see. She puts her hands on her hips, pretending to shout, and points and shakes her fist. I feel a huge laugh inside me, watching Sylvia clown out of the corner of my eye.

"That's fine. Don't expect me to hold dinner," I say in the same low voice. Dennis turns and Sylvia ducks instantly out of sight. He goes to the door. I stand frozen, scowling, laughter trying to explode out of me.

He slams the door and laughter does explode from me. I choke and shriek with it. Tears run down my face. I lean against the window, gasping for breath, watching Dennis sneak into a little red sports car. Sylvia sits behind the steering wheel. Dennis doesn't look back, but Sylvia turns and raises her eyebrows at me. I wave with both hands at her and dance around like a maniac. The car drives away, and I laugh for another minute, standing in the living room without Dennis there or anywhere around, just laughing, alone, laughing so hard that for several moments I don't stop being there, even without Dennis, his needs, his story.

That is the only time I laugh for a long time. My scenes stay short and angry. I suspect most of Dennis's story is somewhere else. Maybe with Sylvia. I am happy to think she's out there, somewhere, maybe clowning behind his back, but I never catch a glimpse of her. Fighting with Dennis was tedious the first time, but it's all that happens for me.

And I can't steal any more time for myself. When Dennis goes, I try to hang on. I promise myself a reward if I can do it. The problem is, I can't think what I could give myself. I think Sylvia must know something I don't. She was there that time, when Dennis didn't know it. How did she do that?

Somewhere within a scene break we have moved to a house, but it's the only thing that's changed. Dennis may be a little older. I probably am, too, but there are no mirrors in the rooms in which we fight.

This is the best I can do:

"You are a shrew," Dennis says.

My hands are wrapped loosely inside a big dish towel. "Who made me one?" I say. Inside the towel, I dance my fingers around crazily. He doesn't know I'm doing it.

Dennis is stomping away to the door, and I have seen this before, and before, and before.

When his back is to me I drop the dish towel and twirl around three times on my toes—in the few moments before he gets to the door and it's over again.

ooo

"I called her," I say to him. I called someone? I want to cheer. It's different. I have an active role in this fight.

"Who?"

"Your tramp," I say. I think that means Sylvia. I wish it hadn't happened off scene. I wish it was something I had done, rather than something I tell Dennis about. "I invited her for dinner."

"My god, Emmy, you didn't. There's nothing going on between us and you know it, and you're going to throw some kind of hysterical scene!"

"I don't see how you can have any objection to inviting one of your friends for dinner. I'm always alone and starved for company in this house." I wish this were true. I am always with Dennis, only with Dennis. I don't exist alone. "Maybe now you'll stay home for dinner one time."

"You're not going to do this," he says.

"She said she'd come, and she'll be here in half an hour. I have to finish making the gravy," I say. I go to the kitchen and stir brown stuff in a long flat pan on the stove. There is a heavy silence from the living room. It's very much like being alone. I like the feel of the wooden spoon in my hand. It feels more and more real as I move it through the thick brown sauce. I can feel the wood grain against my palm. I hold it firmly, its growing reality, thinking about nothing but the spoon.

I take the gravy off the stove when the doorbell rings and go to join Dennis, greeting Sylvia at the door. I can tell when I see her that we are all older. Maybe ten, maybe fifteen years older. She's beautiful.

"Hello, Emmy," says Sylvia. Her voice is a little lower than it was in the gym.

She hands me her coat. Her dress looks like one of the ones in the lingerie catalog I was shouting at Dennis about many scenes back. Then I don't look at her. I want to, but my face turns away. "Hello, Sylvia," I say flatly. "Dinner's almost ready."

"Maybe we can catch up on old times while it finishes," she says in a voice just as flat. Dennis looks upset. Sylvia and I walk back in the house to the den.

My heart is beating hard as I shut the door behind us. I am afraid the scene will break. My hands lock the door and it makes a loud click, loud enough to be heard down the hall. I can hear the floor creak from Dennis's step. He often paces when we're about to argue.

I turn to Sylvia. She whoops a whispered whoop and throws her arms around me in a hug that knocks my feet off the floor. "Time!" she whispers, picking me up. "We have time!"

"How much time?" I whisper, rubbing my sore bottom, a part of myself I think I've never felt before. "How long can this scene last until we have to go out there again?" Then, "Slut!" I shout. I pick up a lamp and throw it at the wall. It shatters loudly.

Sylvia giggles. Her high cheeks flush with merriment. "We're having a fight in here," she whispers. "How ridiculous! –Do you know the trick?"

"The trick?" I say, confused.

"To make time last."

I don't know what she's talking about.

"When he's not paying close attention to you, when the story's not paying close attention to you–when he's not *looking* at you, it doesn't matter what you're doing," she says. I make shapes with my fingers, remembering. "So it doesn't matter how much time *you* think is passing. You can decide for yourself how much time it is."

She grins. "Once when he went to the bathroom, I took the whole stereo apart. To see how it worked. When I decided I was finished and he came out, it all went back together again. I took a bicycle apart once too. It was easier to figure out." She's talking very fast, like she's stored things up to tell me. "I think I stole an hour, or two hours, just while he was taking a leak. I probably could have taken more, but there just wasn't anything to do once I had all those pieces laid out. Hotel rooms are boring. Haven't you done anything like that?"

"I'm never alone in a room," I say. "It's a fight, and another fight, and another fight. Nothing in between."

"No. Not even once?"

"Once I laughed, all by myself," I say, remembering.

"Tell me what you've done. Tell me what you've thought."

I tell her about my part of the story, what it's like to be the shrewish wife to a person I don't really know, how I've tried to fit the story together from the little pieces I've seen and decided it wasn't good or fair. I am too embarrassed to tell her how often I think about her.

"Excuse me a second," whispers Sylvia. She knocks over a leather chair and squeals a loud outraged squeal: "*You—*!" The floor creaks again outside.

I sit on the floor against the overturned chair. I clutch my knees and start to cry. The tears feel natural, and bitter.

"Hush," says Sylvia. "Hush." She kneels down next to me. She puts her arms around me. "Hush, honey, hush." She brushes my hair back with her fingers. I reach out to feel her own long, gold hair. It is soft and heavy. She kisses a tear off my cheek. I reach my hand down behind her neck.

Sylvia is so strong, the sort of person you know you can only admire. I start to pull away. She catches my hand.

"You're real," she whispers. "You see things. You think things. You're so beautiful." She brings my hand up and kisses my fingers. She kisses me on the lips. I find the way her dress unfastens, and I pull it away to see what all of her looks like. I run my hand from her neck down to her hip, along the warm curves of her side. She moves her arms gracefully, pulling my blouse up.

I want to tell everything and leave nothing out. I do not mean to leave anything out when I say: I do not now do anything that I have not thought to do. What Sylvia does is what she thinks of herself. It feels beautiful. It feels real. And I stop waiting for another creak outside the room. I forget for a long time that there is an outside the room.

We lie there together a long time, breathing quietly and not having to do anything we don't want to, most of the time. Once I have to slap my hands together hard, and Sylvia has to cry out. Her eye swells and starts to turn dark underneath.

"I wish I got hurt instead of you," I whisper.

"It doesn't hurt."

Finally I start to drowse, and that must be when time starts fast again. Dennis has forced the door open, and I am standing with my hand raised to Sylvia. There is a smirk on her mouth, but her eyes are kind and searching. She looks like she wants to tell me something. Dennis shoves me and takes Sylvia out of the room. I don't think he's coming back in this scene. I will myself not to go away. I will being alone in this room.

I sit beside the overturned leather chair and feel it, its grain different from the wooden spoon, different from Sylvia's skin. I compare the feeling of all three textures, wood and leather and skin, and I love them all. I stroke the chair and

Dennis doesn't talk to me now. There are no fights. There is silence. Bits of silence in fast patches, as he enters and leaves, enters and leaves, once or twice glowers through breakfast or dinner. In the silences, I think about my memories, and at the moments of his leaving I practice making time for myself out of his inattention.

I learn how. I make a lot of time.

I duck into the room in which Sylvia and I were together when we had the fight for his benefit, and I fix it up. I take the curtains off the windows so all the sun comes in. I don't worry about privacy, because there is never anyone outside the window, though I keep looking. I put the leather chair in the middle of the sunlight, so that it is warmer than a person, soft in the sun. I take books off the shelves to read them, but there are no words inside; so I take their bright jackets off and put them on the walls. Later I sneak in the kitchen scissors and cut the jackets into colorful shapes, flowers and birds and bright red mouths. I cover the walls with paper kisses.

I'd like to write in the empty books, but all I know is the story I am in, and I don't even know most of it. Just what I see from where I am.

The parts of the story I am in become more fractioned, more disjointed. Dennis walks into the room, throws his jacket on a chair, and walks out. Dennis shouts at me that he cannot take off work for a vacation. Dennis comes home late, drunk, and does not say a word. Dennis ages faster, scene by scene. The story must end when he dies, if not before that. Time is precious. I make my own hours for every few seconds of time with him.

In my time, I cut the curtains in my room into long shreds and sew them together to make a huge floral robe that swirls around me when I move. I exercise my memory: I remember seeing a boy sail

127

a paper airplane in the first moments of my life, and I tear pages out of books and fold them until I get something that flies. The failed shapes I hang by thread from the ceiling so they won't have to be failures. When the weather is warm so I can open the window (one day it will be spring, the next, winter, the next, summer) they swing against each other, rustling.

Always I tire, lose my concentration and find myself in another fragmentary moment with Dennis.

He is reading the paper one time when I see a little red car drive by. It has dents and rust on it. I see Dennis see the car, too; his eyes flick up, and then he looks back down at the paper. Dennis shows no emotion now.

The instant he looks down I run into the kitchen and out the back door, where I've never been before. The back yard is an expanse of hazy green, without detail. I run around the house and wave frantically at the back of the car.

Sylvia pulls over, out of the view of our front window. I climb in. She is wide and round now, her hair more gray than gold. She looks good. I hug her.

"I've missed you," I say. "I've taken a lot of time for myself. I've fixed up the room. You'll think it's silly. Come and see."

"I've had no time since I saw you," she says. "One little bit with Dennis telling me it was over, but that was it—that was the one moment I've had since I was here last. I think I'm out of the story."

"I thought you *were* the story! I thought that was it—Dennis going back and forth between the two of us."

She shakes her head. There is a little gray curling around one ear. I want to touch it, so I do. "I don't think it has anything much to do with either of us. I think it has more to do with his job, now, and I'd bet he's selling secrets. Now that he doesn't have a home life or a mistress, I think he'll go further and further until he's caught."

"His job? I don't know anything about it! What could be interesting about that?"

"Who knows? We're just peripheral to it all."

I am angry. "All this mucking about to make a life for him, and it doesn't even have anything to do with us!"

"Poor Dennis," says Sylvia.

"Poor Dennis?"

She shakes her head. "He's so trapped."

"So are—"

She puts both arms around me and holds me, her breath in my hair. "We have room to make up parts of ourself. Room to live, in the cracks of this story. What does he have? Does he get to wonder? We can't even ask him. He can't even tell us." Her voice is rich with sympathy. I remember all over again how fine a person she is. I snuggle against her, feeling peaceful.

Later, when I ask, she gets out of the car and dances with me. There is no one on the street, no one on the sidewalk. She dances barefoot on the featureless grass, bending and reaching, slowly, with a kind of dignity that is new. Her body is mature, full, now. We dance to no music with the wind in our faces. Then we lie on the grass and look up. "I never saw clouds before," I say.

"Look closely," she says. "I think the story's almost over. You may never see them again." I turn on my elbow to her, but she is looking up at the sky. "You may never see me again, either."

"No!" I cry. "That can't happen—I've hardly seen you!"

"Things end." Blue sky reflects in her eyes. "This has been the best part. With you."

"Stories can be told again." If I say it firmly, I might believe it.

She smiles with her mouth and glances at me. "This isn't our story. We stole what we have." Her mouth quirks sideways and she looks back up. "When this story gets told again it's just Dennis's sad little life, starting high and selling out until he ruins himself. No happy ending. If he doesn't get one, why should we expect to?"

I want to cry, but I can tell she is close to it herself, and Sylvia is not a person who likes to cry. I lean over her and kiss her neck, in her favorite spot.

Time does not stretch forever. In the end Sylvia is back in the car driving out of sight, and I go back to the living room behind Dennis's back. I think I see a flash of light from her bumper as I hear the sound of her engine fade away. There has been no goodbye. She never saw my room.

Dennis folds his paper. "I have to go to the office."

"On a Sunday?" my voice says. None of the loss of Sylvia I feel in it: the tired resignation of a wife nagging her husband for the thousandth time.

"Things are complicated, all right?" he snaps. Suddenly I know it is almost over. Shaken, I forget to steal time.

Dennis is home, ashen, something terrible happening he won't talk about. I know Sylvia was right and I will never see her again. She is gone. Soon I will be too.

The phone rings and Dennis answers it, panic and wheedling, not words, audible in his muttering. I leave him on the phone and go back into my room. Lopsided paper birds fly under the ceiling. My robe is spread across the chair. If Dennis came into this room, would everything that is mine in it vanish?

It will all vanish soon anyway.

I look out the window, wanting to see her car. The road is not visible from here.

Now I cry, the first time I have ever really cried, myself, not Dennis's little wife Emmy in the story. I pull my flower robe up around my face and sob, silently. Dennis must not hear me. It could break the last time I can make my own time.

I cry until I get angry. I did not decide on my life. I did not write it. I tear off the robe and start yanking hangings from the ceiling, furious that they are all I have done with my life, furious that Sylvia never even saw them, furious that they are foolish. I think if she did see them, she'd laugh at them. I can hear her laughter in my mind.

But my mind can't make it mocking. Even when she made fun of Dennis, there was nothing hurtful in it.

I think of Sylvia, laughing. I'm the only one who knew her, and soon I will be gone. The story could be told again with nowhere any trace of me, of Sylvia. Only Dennis and the fleeting images of women in his life. Only Dennis's story.

I barely knew Sylvia, but knowing her made her more real, as her knowing me freed me. My anger falls away. My frustration falls away. Sylvia found ways around the limitations. I remember her laugh.

I push the leather chair over to the writing desk. My body has gotten older and the chair is heavy; I sweat doing it, and like the feel of my sweat. I open the drawer and find some pens. I take down two books and open the first one to a fresh, white piece of paper, clean, like Sylvia's grin. I gather my memories around me, with the cutouts and the hangings and my tattered funny robe. They all belong to me.

I write on the cloth cover of the first book, "The Story So Far." I write on the cover of the second, "The Further Adventures of Sylvia and Emmy." In the first book, I begin:

"We grew up in the same small town, in the same short story. . . ."

When I finish this story, I will start the new one.

The Spinner

Rianna lived alone on the other side of the hill outside town. Each month she went down into town to bargain for wool of sheep, hair of goat, for flax and cotton. Each day she spun them into yarn and thread. Each week she took what she had spun and sold it to one of several women who wove it into cloth they themselves sold. She had moved to this town two years ago, when her mother died, because her own had too many spinners. The hillside was pretty, and she was busy and content.

Rianna traded with a dressmaker for her clothes. She knew herself to be a poor cook, and her housekeeping was none too good. She spun only, but she could spin anything human hands could spin.

When she tired of spinning wool, goathair, and flax, she would spin other things, just for her fun: fur from the coats of her sleepy dog and of the two fat fluffy cats who slept at his flanks; hair from the manes of horses; fibers she pulled from the drying pods of plants that grew along the edge of the swamp. Not all of these made supple yarn or strong thread, but most of what she spun from them she was able to sell or trade.

It was spun dog and cat fur that brought Rowan to her door.

"Spinner, can you spin me gold?" he asked. A bag, full and light, was slung over his back.

She did not know him, but she had seen him, sometimes, at a distance, walking through the hills at twilight. She recognized him by the fine fair hair that swirled around his shoulders in the strong afternoon breeze. He was a woodcutter who came to town less often than she.

"That is just an old story," she said.

He grinned. His eyes were hazel. "That's too bad, for gold is what

I need." He swung his bag to her doorstep and opened it. "What can you do with this?"

It was full of the pods of a plant she had not seen before. She took one and pulled lint from it. It was very light and fine, and shone in the sun like the woodcutter's hair. "Where did you get these?"

"They grow deep in the woods, where I sometimes go to cut old, thick trees," he said. "My name is Rowan. They tell me you are Rianna the spinner, and you can spin anything."

"Everything I have tried," she said. She twisted and pulled the plantstuff; she spun it between her fingers to look at the thread it made.

"I have seen a shawl knitted from your dog-fur yarn. Someone bought that. Would someone buy this, if you spun it?"

"Perhaps," Rianna said. She liked the look of the lint. She took the bag and went to her wheel. The lint pulled easily from the pods. In a minute or two she had enough to wrap around the distaff. She spun. The thread shone on the spool.

"Pretty enough," she said, "but none too strong." She thought a moment, then tsk-tsked to her cats until one came. She took the purring animal in her lap and combed long brown fur from it. "This is a trick I have played with before," she said. The fur went around the distaff with what the woodcutter had brought, and she spun the two together. The yarn wound onto the spindle and she nodded.

"Better," she said.

"What can we sell it for?" he asked.

"Whatever people will pay for it. Why do you want gold so much, woodcutter?"

"There is a maid in town I would marry," he said. "She will have me, but her father will not let her go to a man who has only his axe and a cabin he built with his own hands, strong as that cabin may be. If I show him gold in my hand, and perhaps some for his purse, he will show me his blessing."

He was straight and strong and warm of eye. Rianna could see how a town girl might be willing to move to a dark cottage in the woods for that warmth. "I will need many more of these plants," she said. "Do you have animals?"

"Cats," he said. "Why?"

"If we use mine, I take a larger share of the gold," said Rianna.

The woodcutter grinned again. "You'll do it."

"And you will have to wash and soak the lint," she said, standing from her stool. "It is not a job I like. I can show you how."

The woodcutter laughed and swept her up in his arms. She blinked at him, startled. "We will be great partners," he said, releasing her. "It's a fair day brought me to your door." Rianna tilted her head to see the cloudy sky, and smiled at the woodcutter's back as he strode down her walk.

Rowan had five cats, all of a litter and all pale orange. In a few weeks' time he brought their fur to her, and many bags more of the woodland pods. The cat fur was long and seemed to wind through Rianna's fingers of itself. She spun thread that shone like gold. The woodcutter came to her door at odd hours late in the evening, gave her a bag or two, and left.

Rianna took some of the thread to the weaver. The cloth it yielded was lovely, and, as it did not need to be dyed, would never dull in color. A merchant's wife said she would take enough to make two gowns.

The season passed and she had as much lint as she could want, and not enough fur to go with it. Still the woodcutter came from time to time. He would sit by the fire and watch her spin, as she carefully admixed the one fiber with the other to keep color and texture true.

"You are a marvel," he said. "Truly you could spin anything."

"Anything I have tried," she said again, and they laughed together. It was now an old joke between them.

"You spin gold," he said. "It is gold to the eye, we will have gold for it, it is gold. You have spun out the most precious stuff, all to help me."

"I'll take my share," she said.

"We share everything."

"Half and half," she said.

"Half and half," he said, and kissed her.

Rianna's lips warmed to his, but she remembered, and said, "You have a maid in town."

"Not now."

Not anymore, or not yet? Rianna wondered, as the woodcutter

reached up and unpinned her plaited red hair; he pulled her hair loose and she was unspun. She fell into his arms like a tree.

Each night the woodcutter came to her until spring, when his cats gave off fur. Now she spun the last of the golden thread; now they carted it together to the weaver, receiving for their labors two small bags of coins.

Rowan did not come back to watch her spin, not that night, nor the next. She thought she should go to see him, until a farmer told her, as he piled wool down from his cart, that a wedding was being planned in town. "A woodcutter and a merchant's daughter, imagine that."

"Imagine that," Rianna said. Her fingers felt numb, counting out coins. "Imagine that." The thought of tall Rowan dancing at his wedding with a giggling town girl filled her mind. She wished that she could not imagine it. "When is the wedding?"

"In six, no, in seven weeks' time, I hear," said the farmer chattily. He waited for a response Rianna could not make.

The next day she spun from the time she roused herself in the morning until late into the night, when her eyes stung and her head was heavy. It was working so that made her eyes sting. She spun without ceasing for a week and another, dust building unnoticed in her cottage, hair slack and unplaited to her waist, and then she had nothing left to spin.

And still Rowan had not come to say goodbye.

Rianna could not sleep, she could not eat. "It is not fair," she thought, "that he forgets me. He may leave me and abandon our partnership, our friendship and our pleasure, but he should not forget me." The thought persisted in her mind like a knot she could not undo. She brushed her dog until it yelped and cried and her cats until they hissed and clawed, seeking more wool to spin, but she could not keep herself busy.

The weaver came to her cottage. "When will you have more golden thread?" she asked. "All the women in town ask about it, with the merchant's wife showing off the golden dress she'll wear at her daughter's wedding."

"Is that who bought the dress?" Rianna asked.

"It is," said the weaver. "But we will not sell the cloth so cheaply again. The merchant has shown the cloth to a visiting noble from the court. I told him if he would have more to sell to them, it would cost at least twice what he paid before. He did not flinch. Will you spin more thread for me?"

"I cannot," said Rianna.

The weaver frowned. "Do not hold back on me now, girl," she said. "We have been together from the start. The merchant made his bargain with me."

"I cannot," Rianna said again. Rowan no longer brought the plants he found deep in the woods. Rowan no longer came at all.

"If you cannot bring me that thread," said the weaver, "see if I buy any thread from you again. Everyone spins. One spinner less means nothing."

By the next week Rianna still had nothing to spin. She went to town, hair bound carelessly and skirts hanging crooked. She discovered the weaver had spread stories she was mad, that she had made a dark bargain for her skills. No one would look at her eye to eye.

"I am not mad," she thought. "But if I cannot work, I will be mad before the summer is out." She went from farm to farm in bare feet and trampled skirts to plead for flax and wool. From farm to farm she was turned away.

She found herself, near night, in the fringe of the woods, at the door to Rowan's cabin. Her rap was so faint it could barely be heard, but he opened the door and looked at her silently.

"They will not let me spin," she said. "They want the golden thread. They think I am mad. Without your pods I have nothing. Without you I do not sleep. You must help me find the pods."

"I am preparing for my wedding," said the woodcutter. "I have no time to hunt for pods."

"You know the woods and I do not. You must help me," she said. "With all that was between us."

"There was nothing between us." Rowan's voice was mild. "We have split the gold and our business is done."

"Something is yet between us," said Rianna.

"Go home," he said. "You can spin anything, spinner. Find something else to spin." He shut the door firmly.

The sun was nearly down and Rianna stumbled on her way to her cottage, cutting her feet and bruising her shins. In the dark she finally reached her home; in sobs she fell beside her wheel. She had nothing left to spin. She had nothing left. She had nothing but the ache in her heart and the memory of what was gone and foolish.

She turned her wheel.

She went to her little dresser and took a hairbrush from the lowest drawer. In it were caught Rowan's fair golden hairs amid her red ones. She brought it to the wheel and spun the hairs all together. They made the barest thread. But she could not stop spinning. Memories seemed to flow from her fingers. She spun how he had touched her, she spun how he had whispered to her, she spun how he had cried out. She spun her hopes and she spun her joys and she spun her tears. She could spin anything, and they were all she had to spin. She spun until the dawn.

There was nothing to see upon the wheel, not even the fair golden hairs or the red ones, but she took what she could not see between her fingers and twisted it upon itself. She twisted a cord of love and need, pain and want.

She tied one end of the cord to her wrist, wound the rest around her forearm, and went again to Rowan's cabin. He was not there. She pulled a handful of her red hair and tied it around the handle of his door, and went home to wait.

That afternoon Rowan came to her door. "I found this around my door handle," he said. He held the lock of red hair. "My future father-in-law came visiting and asked what it was." He threw the hair to the floor. "Stay away from my home. Our lives have gone their two ways and there is nothing between us, spinner. Forget me."

Rianna unspooled invisible cord from her forearm and grabbed the woodcutter's wrist. He made one startled noise before she tied the cord above his hand. Her unsteady heart took a new jump at the moment she knotted the knot.

"If there is nothing between us, then go," she said.

"I will," he whispered. He turned to leave. He took three steps. He stopped.

"Ah, Rianna!" he cried out. "Ah, what is it you have done to me?" He turned back to her, his eyes wide and wild.

"Go," she said, with difficulty, each memory of the two of them sharper and more painful than ever before. "Go, now, if you can!"

"I cannot go," he said. His breath was ragged. "God help me but I cannot." He caught her face in his hands and kissed it. He fell shaking at her feet.

She took him into her cottage and in time made him stop weeping. She promised he would not have to leave.

Three paces was the length of the cord. From that moment Rowan did not depart three steps from her side. At times, when he turned or rose or sat, she thought she could see a glint of gold wind from his wrist to hers. At times, out of the corner of her eye, she thought she saw it growing deeper into the flesh of his arm.

Three days he wept at odd moments. Three nights he called the name of another woman in his deepest sleep. Three mornings he woke and stared at Rianna as though wondering who she was. Each morning she kissed him until the confusion slipped from his eyes, replaced with need, and then with hope, and then with trust. Each day he wept less. Each night he called out another woman's voice less frequently. And then, at last, he breathed only, "Rianna."

Another week she kept the woodcutter at her side. For long hours he would lay his head on her lap and she would stroke his hair, feeling a peace she hadn't known before. She did not spin and did not miss it. She had enough gold to buy food for a year.

But she did not forget why she had spun him to her. After three days and a week she said, "Rowan, do you love me?"

"Ah, God, Rianna, I cannot live without you. You go through and down to the bottom of me. Ah, Rianna, I do not understand how I did not see it before. I will always love you."

She had spun the man to her. She could spin anything.

Now he had started talking, he would not stop. Every word he said, her heart echoed. "We can live on love. Surely we can live on love. And if we have need of anything else, we can go to the woods together and gather that plant, and you can spin it for gold. But never leave my side, Rianna. You cannot leave me."

He was the man who had broken her heart. He was the man on whom she planned revenge. He was the man she could love for the rest of her life. She picked up her heavy shears.

"You must never go," he said.

"I will go if I can," she said, and marveled at how steady her hand was as she cut the invisible cord between them. All color left Rowan's face, and he collapsed to the floor.

"You cannot leave," he said hoarsely. "I cannot let you go. Rianna!"

She knew that he would never recover from her, and that now she could never recover from him.

"There is nothing between us," she said.

She turned and walked from her cottage; and she never returned in her lifetime or yours.

Good Girl,
Bad Dog

Not-Timmy smells bad, sticky with chocolate and anger. He does not want to be near not-Timmy, but Trainer is there making him. Not-Timmy looks furiously past the camera at the humans standing together there, then puts on a sweet smile and reaches down to pet his ears, pulling them.

"Good girl," not-Timmy says.

He is not a girl. He is not a bitch. He is a Dog.

Trainer stands away from the camera and other humans. He makes a signal with his hand.

"Woof!" says the Dog. His ears hurt. Later he will get a biscuit. He smells not-Timmy and feels the hot lights sting his eyes and wonders if it is enough.

Not-Timmy's trainer watches intently, making a signal to the boy with his eyes. "Ha ha ha!" says not-Timmy, loud like a bark. "Ha ha ha!" say the bigger humans standing on this side of the camera with not-Timmy. The humans on the other side of the camera say nothing. The human-trainer has not signaled them.

The human-trainer will give not-Timmy a biscuit, one that smells like chocolate instead of grain and stale meat juices. The Dog does not know what the bigger humans get. There are many of them and some are stronger than the human-trainer, so it must be something very big.

"Cut!" says the human-trainer. The hot lights go off. The humans from behind the camera walk away. Not-Timmy lets go of the Dog's ears and runs off. "Timmy!" yells the human-trainer. When the human-trainer is not standing behind the camera, most people call not-Timmy by a different name, but the human-trainer still calls him Timmy.

The name they call the Dog is the same all the time, with the camera or without the camera. It is a wrong name. It is a bitch's name. It goes with saying "Good girl!" and he is not a girl. He will not use the name in his own mind.

He is a Dog. Sometimes he dreams he is Wolf.

Trainer had a wolf once.

The wolf was gray and sleek, where the Dog had ruffs of pale soft fur. Wolf fur was thick and rough, at least to sight, for the wolf was locked in a kennel behind the Dog's, and the Dog could not get close enough even to smell him properly.

What he could smell even through bars and great distance was hatred of Trainer and kennels and commands and stale biscuits. The wolf would never let anyone call him a bitch and say "Good girl!" and pull his ears. The Dog imagined the wolf tearing Trainer's throat out. He dreamed it, and it made him whimper in his sleep, but he always hoped to dream the dream again. Sometimes he still dreams it.

Trainer did not keep the wolf for long. Maybe Trainer took him away and killed him before he could kill Trainer, with a heavy stick in his human hands; for the Dog cannot imagine Trainer's small shouting mouth at the wolf's throat.

"Come," says Trainer, using the bitch-name the Dog will not hear but must answer to.

The Dog does not want to come. The Dog puts on his alert face, the way he has been taught: head cocked, ears up, sitting straight.

"Come, damn it!" Trainer raises his hand.

The Dog decides. He makes a break for it, ducking between cables and kitchen walls that end in the middle and the shifting legs of humans. He has knocked the camera over: he can hear it landing in a noisy crash of metal and glass as Trainer shouts at him.

Trainer shouts many words the Dog has never heard before. They are very easy not to respond to. Harder is when Trainer shouts "Come!" and "Bad!" Years of hearing these words, food when he does what Trainer says, shouts when he does not, have made them very, very big. These words try to pull his shoulders down into a guilty cringe. They are harder to run past than the set walls and the humans trying to grab for him.

But the Dog does run past them. He is a Bad Dog. He is not a Good Girl.

He is like the wolf.

He is so excited, he wants to piss on the whole set, on all the human things, to mark it all as his, the Bad Dog's. But humans are still grabbing at him, and he knows he can not stop now. To decide to be a Bad Dog is to go and keep going, all the way, like a wolf after prey.

Behind the set walls are many cables and boxes and poles and boards. It is a maze the humans are clumsy in, but a Bad Dog can run through quickly, knocking more things back in the humans' path. Soon the Dog is away from all the sounds of shouting. He keeps running. He will reach the wild. He will be a Wild Dog, a collie wolf.

He knows where the wild is. They film on it. The wild is where not-Timmy falls into a cave and the Good Girl has to stand and bark for the big humans, in front of a camera and both trainers. It is not so far from the set.

It is not so long before he is there, breathing hard but feeling alive, in the wild, not in the kennel and not on the set, no Trainer to yell at him. The wild is a small canyon, scrub and brush, a few trees. The cameras are not there to make it human. Wolves would live here. He throws back his head and howls.

The wild smells tantalizingly of rabbits, but to the Dog's chagrin, he has not been able to chase one down. It is hard to be Wolf when you have been kept in a kennel, trained to fetch and bark on cue instead of hunt. One rabbit after another, prey gets away. He smells around for another one.

There is a sour smell of chocolate and tears. He creeps silently to find the source.

Not-Timmy is sitting on a rock crying.

Not-Timmy can tell the bigger humans where the Bad Dog is. The Dog thinks. He thinks hard, but before he can finish thinking, not-Timmy suddenly turns around and looks at him.

Not-Timmy exclaims, calling him by the bitch-name. The Dog buries a growl in the back of his throat. He has never liked the small human, the way the boy pulls his ears, squeezes him too hard when the human-trainer tells him to Hug, says "Good girl!" in his high, shrill voice. The Dog takes a step back. How could he think real wild would be so close to set and city?

"How did you find me?" not-Timmy says. These are words he would say in front of the camera and the human-trainer. The Dog looks around to see if all the humans are there, if he has run into a trap the humans made. But there are no other humans, just the boy.

Trying to decide what to do, the Dog sits up and puts on his alert face.

What not-Timmy says next is not from his trainer's script, does not sound like the words the human-trainer makes him say. "I hate them all," he says to the Dog. "I hate them making me work, I hate them taking my money, I hate them treating me like I'm just some kid when I work as hard as any of them. If they're gonna treat me like just some kid, they should let me act like just some kid."

The Dog does not know these words, but he knows this is not what the bigger humans make not-Timmy say for them. Not-Timmy smells different, now. Through the chocolate smell, he smells a little like the wolf did. Angry. Fierce.

Maybe not-Timmy is a Bad Boy.

The Dog creeps up and licks his face. It tastes like salt, a little sour. The Dog likes salt. He licks some more.

"Oh, girl!" not-Timmy cries, wrapping his bony arms around the Dog's ruffed shoulders. "Did you run away too? We can run away from those bastards together." He sniffles into the Dog's fur. The Dog does not pull away and run off. The Dog has to think.

The Dog takes not-Timmy to a cave in which they've filmed before. Not-Timmy was in that scene, but he didn't seem to remember where the cave was. Not-Timmy is not good at being wild. When the Dog shows him the cave, not-Timmy cries "Good girl!", and the Dog tries not to snarl. He is not here to be a Good Girl. Not-Timmy should know better.

They stay in the cave while it gets dark, and gets light, and gets dark again. Not-Timmy talks a lot. The Dog tries not to listen to his piercing voice. By second dark the Dog is getting very hungry, and not-Timmy has started to whine. The Dog knows whines. The kennel was full of them.

"They'll be missing me by now," the boy says. "They've got to be sorry by now. Serve them right if I never came back. See what happens to their show without its star. Serve them right if I never came back, but I can't stay here. They've had their scare. They'll treat me right, now. I'm starving. I'm thirsty. I'm going to go home."

"Go Home" are human words the Dog understands. He has been dozing nearer the front of the cave, away from not-Timmy, but his ears prick high at the sound of the words. "Go Home" means back to the other humans. "Go Home" means be a Good Girl, not wild, not a Bad Dog. Not-Timmy wants him to Go Home. He will not do that. He buries his nose back under his leg. He will starve a Wild Dog, a Bad Dog, rather than eat another of Trainer's biscuits.

Not-Timmy has got up and grabbed his small pack. It had chocolate in it, which the boy finished eating before first dark. The pack is empty now, but humans carry their possessions everywhere instead of marking them and leaving them. Not-Timmy is going to leave the cave. He is going to Go Home. He is going to bring humans back to find the Bad Dog. Trainer will hit the Dog with a stick, and maybe tear his throat out. If he does not tear his throat out, he will make him be a Good Girl, make him Sit and Fetch and Stay and sleep in the kennel.

The Dog leaps at not-Timmy as the boy reaches the cave entrance. He knocks not-Timmy over the way he knocked the camera over, but not-Timmy sounds different from the camera as he lands on the rocky cave floor: there is a thud, a small snapping sound, and a sudden sharp cry.

"Shit!" cries the boy, clutching his leg. "It's broken!" He whimpers like a puppy. The Dog sits looking at him, not knowing what to do now.

"Get help," says not-Timmy. "Go get help. Go home. Tell the director. Tell anyone! Get help!"

The Dog knows many of these words. They do this in the scripts all the time. He runs off, he runs back with a big human, or, if a big human is the one lying on the ground saying Get Help, with not-Timmy; and when the camera stops whirring Trainer gives him biscuits. If Trainer were here, he would be signaling the Dog when to look alert, when to touch not-Timmy with one paw, when to turn and run away from not-Timmy and the camera. This is the game the humans play.

The Dog looks at not-Timmy clutching his leg and weeping. He raises his ears and cocks his head.

"Yes, girl, that's it! Get help! Get help!"

The Dog puts his paw gently on not-Timmy's arm.

"Good girl!" says the boy. His eyes plead, full of pain and hope. The Dog can smell it on his sour human skin.

The Dog takes not-Timmy by the collar of his shirt and drags him back into the far recesses of the cave.

By next light he is not hungry anymore.

The little girl has wandered far away from her family's picnic, and she is lost and tired from crying about it.

She hears a little sound and looks up, startled. It is a friendly collie face. She's seen it on television. It's just like television! She'll be saved now! She calls the dog by name and it comes right up to her and licks her face. Just like television.

"Good doggy, good girl, are you going to take me back to my mommy and daddy now?"

The collie pricks up its ears, cocks its head in a comical manner, and leads the little girl away from the way she came, further into the canyon, back into a sheltered cave.

The rabbits in the wilds of Los Angeles may be difficult prey, but a Bad Dog—a Wolf—can get by.

Absent Friends

It was a mistake getting the tree. Douglas's hands were scraped and sore, and his joints ached from spending too much time wrestling with the thing in the damp, steady wind. Ten minutes just to get it up the stairs to his second-floor apartment.

Ah, well, but an Iowa winter would surely kill him. That, or his parents' cutting concern. Better to take his chances with San Francisco, and loneliness, and Mrs. Aguilar downstairs.

On cue, she started with the broomstick, banging it on her ceiling. *Bang, bang. Bang, bang.* He had provoked her by dragging a heavy Christmas tree up past her door at nine at night. He had provoked her with the noise of his grunts as he wrestled it up the stairs, and with the scattered pine needles he was too exhausted to sweep off the stairs. He always provoked her, with his friends, his hours, his clothes, his inability to understand Spanish, his pallor and thinness. His existence.

The first hadn't troubled her for some time, and the last shouldn't trouble her much longer.

He sat very still, waiting. If she didn't use the broomstick for more than a few seconds, she usually didn't go on to call the cops. The tree lay on its side across from his worn sofa, filling a third of the space in his living room. Bedroom. Room. He couldn't put it up tonight, or she would call the cops. By tomorrow it would be half-dead. "Sorry," he told it.

The tree was silent. It was a good neighbor.

Douglas risked getting up and going to the kitchen for a hit of oxygen. He walked carefully in stocking feet, but he could hear the floor creak. Damn. He put the mask over his nose and mouth, turned the valve, took a few deep breaths. He felt a little less dizzy. Had he eaten today? His volunteer would be pissed at him if he hadn't made a dent in his larder next time she came by. Tough love, that's what she was into. Douglas had liked his previous volunteer better, but Ray had got sick, and had to quit. Maybe now Douglas's new volunteer was visiting Ray's house, too. Douglas didn't want to call him. He might call and find out—he might get bad news.

He couldn't put up the tree now, and he couldn't fall asleep for hours, probably not before three or four. He took a jar of crunchy peanut butter and a half-full bag of pretzel sticks and went back into the main room, pushing his feet along without lifting them. The floor creaked.

"Damn it!" Douglas said. He was just sure tonight she'd call the cops.

It was Christmas Eve.

The cops were always nice; they always seemed to guess about his illness; they always left again after talking to Mrs. Aguilar for a time and him for a time, not saying they thought she was crazy, but showing it in their eyes. And pity for him. But it was embarrassing, it rattled him, and he had enough trouble sleeping at night. She'd call tonight, of course she would, because it was just his damn luck.

Don't think about it. He'd worry himself sick. Couldn't afford to. Wouldn't. He sat and unscrewed the jar, the lid rasping hollowly, and jammed a pretzel stick in the peanut butter. The pretzel, when he bit into it, was stale. He'd left the bag open. His feeble excuse for an appetite left him, but he finished the pretzel. There, Margaret, I've eaten, are you happy? he thought. There's half an ounce less I'll have lost at my next checkup.

Oh, hell, even Margaret with all her stubborn volunteer concern wouldn't be thinking about him tonight, wrapped in the bosom of her family in Christmas bliss.

Fine. Enough. He leaned forward in his unfolded futon sofabed, one of two pieces of furniture in this room, to the coffee table. He felt a little dizzy as he reached for the lower shelf. The scent of dying pine in the room was too strong. He grasped for his photo album, found it, and opened it in his lap.

There was a file label stuck to the first page: "Christmas—1958-1981." The page was empty. The next ten pages were empty, front and back. The film over each page showed marks where it had once held down snapshots. Douglas could remember a few. There was a picture of him at two in his grandmother's lap; she had died when he was four. There was one of him at twelve with a blue, adult-size bike. One of him at five in a cowboy suit. Now he knew friends of friends who decked out in cowboy paraphernalia every night they went out, but he didn't think his parents would think that cute. It made him think of himself as a little kid at Christmas, playing with his new plastic six-shooters: not his idea of sexy.

Those photos were gone. He'd ripped them up and thrown them out last year, when his sister said she couldn't possibly come visit. She had to worry about her small children, and whatever the doctors said, how could you be sure? And his parents had supported her. So much for Christmases past. They didn't want him now, he didn't need them then.

Past the blank pages was the label "Auld Lang Syne." These pictures were still there. He wasn't related to anyone in them. They were in no good order: faded pictures of grade-school friends lay side by side with photographs taken only a few years before.

There was Jerry. He was dead. There was Patrick. He was dead. There was Rob. Douglas pursed his lips, considering. He didn't know if Rob was dead. He hadn't seen him in three or four years. Safest to assume he was. There were George and Carlos. Carlos was dead and George had gone home to Mississippi to die. Mississippi had to be a worse place to die than Iowa. Douglas was lucky.

Except he wouldn't go home to Iowa.

"Home? Screw it," Patrick had said. What was it, six years ago? He'd had an enormous party, tinsel and presents and mistletoe, in his flat on Noe, the place that was the envy of most of them, right near the heart of the Castro. Douglas had been living in the Sunset district then. He liked going home to a quiet neighborhood. "This is home and this is family. We can make our own traditions and screw anyone who doesn't want us in theirs." Patrick had had a few.

Who else was at that party? He couldn't remember. That was before any of the gang was sick. A life away. Many lives. All his old Christmases were gone. New Christmases might never come. This could be it. The ultimate, final extent of his Christmas cheer.

Suddenly furious, he threw the album against the wall. Pages came loose and scattered on the floor. Pounding started up beneath his feet.

Douglas sat breathing hard, fists clenched. He wanted to go down and confront the woman. Shout at her. Give her what for. Who was he kidding, though? She could knock him over with one blow, over-weight woman of fifty that she was. Pathetic.

There was a rap on the door. Douglas started. Mrs. Aguilar? She preferred to act as though he didn't exist, assaulting his floor or call-ing the police without ever speaking to him. He stayed still. The pounding had stopped downstairs. The rapping came again from the door.

She had to have run up the stairs. Did she think yelling at him in Spanish would do any good? Maybe she was going to hit him with that broom.

He got uncomfortably to his feet and went to the door. He would speak slowly and maybe she would understand. "Ma'am," he said, opening the door, "please, it's Christmas Eve."

"Ma'am?" said the man at his door. Douglas blinked at him. "Excuse me, but I think I'm as macho as anyone you know, fella."

"Rob?" Carrying a bottle of burgundy. "You're not dead."

Rob gave him an incredulous look. "Well, thanks, Dougy. You're looking good too. Are you going to let me in?"

Embarrassment fought with old irritation at the nickname, with nervous relief at seeing an old friend alive, with the knowledge he was *not* looking good. Douglas gave up on trying to make his mouth work and stepped back from the doorway.

"Hey, a picture show," said Rob. He walked over to the wreck-age of the photo album, bootheels clicking on the wooden floor.

"Um," said Douglas. Rob took off his heavy leather jacket and tossed it at the coffee table. It skidded off and thumped on the floor, zippers jangling. "You have to be careful here. About noise."

"Pal," said Rob, "you don't have to tell me what I have to do."

"It's the downstairs neighbor, she's sort of sensitive and she gets upset. She can't sleep. If there's any noise."

"There's traffic and people playing their radios out there, Dougy, she's going to get upset because someone walks on your floor? Not on Christmas Eve, pal. This is a party."

Douglas sat carefully on the futon bed, hoping Rob would follow his lead and stop pacing the floor. "What are you doing here, Rob?

Where have you been? It's been years."

Rob shrugged. "Hanging out with people." He circled the room, examining the old posters taped to the walls, glancing at the prostrate tree.

"Not anyone I've been hanging out with."

"The looks of things, you haven't been hanging with anyone, Dougy. Hot parties in clubs all over the city, and you sit at home Christmas Eve. Is the dust half an inch thick in here or is it just your mood rubbing off on everything?"

He went past Douglas into the kitchen. The click of his boots on the linoleum was high and sharp. Douglas winced. Rob came back into the living room with two glasses filled with wine. "Good god, man, you've got no two clean glasses the same. Is this why you never invited any of the gang over to your old place? I always thought it was because you were afraid of what your nice straight neighbors would think."

"Jesus, Rob, did you look me up to insult me?"

"Not me, Doug." Rob's voice softened. "I'm just here to spend Christmas Eve." He handed Douglas a root-beer mug. "Look, some wine for you. A toast."

Douglas's wrists ached, holding up the heavy mug nearly topped off with dark red wine. He raised it silently in both hands and let Rob clink his juice glass against it.

"To friends," Rob said.

"Absent friends," Douglas said.

"Absent, hell, what good is that?" Rob said. He took a big gulp from the juice glass. "Let's invite 'em over."

"Rob—"

"How long has it been since we all got together? I ain't seen *you* in ages, just for one."

Didn't he know they were all dead? "Rob, you can't."

"Can and did," Rob said. "Ran into an old high-school buddy of yours. It's what made me think of coming over to start out with, when we found out we knew you in common. He's on his way. Had further to come."

"Who?"

"Billy McElroy." Douglas vaguely remembered a skinny blond kid he thought was Billy. "You know he told me he never knew you were gay? What a missed opportunity."

"What, you mean?"

"You didn't know either?" Rob shook his head. "Typical. Well, here's your big chance. So romantic, reunited across the years—"

Douglas was losing patience. "You never change."

Rob stopped and looked at him. "Not anymore," he said. He looked like he would say something else. "Wait, there's the door." He trotted across the room, his steps echoing like gunshots from the walls. This time maybe it *was* Mrs. Aguilar, and Rob would talk to her and make things so much worse. Douglas drank several long swallows of wine.

"Billy, man, glad you could make it!"

"I wasn't doing anything else. I'm glad to be here. That is, if Doug even remembers who I am—"

"You bet he does. The one that got away. All he can talk about, poor sap. Come in, come in!"

Rob escorted the newcomer inside, arm around his shoulder. Billy looked much as Douglas would have expected him to, thicker around the middle and thinner on the top. A little uncomfortable. He was shy, back in school. Billy shook free of Rob's arm, removed his jacket, and draped it quietly across the coffee table.

"Let me get you a drink, Billy," Rob said. "I'm sure I can find a Flintstone glass or something."

Douglas put his mug down and stood up to shake hands. "Um, hi, Billy. Long time."

"Yeah," said Billy. He looked around, and finally sat awkwardly on the coffee table. "Nice tree."

"I should have picked a smaller one." Douglas shrugged, self-conscious. "It's too big for me."

"Thought you liked 'em that way, Dougy boy!" Rob shouted from the kitchen.

"Are you just going to leave it lying there?" Billy asked.

"I have this downstairs neighbor," he said. "If there's any noise at night she goes ballistic." It sounded stupider every time he explained it. It was better than saying he was too weak and tired to put up a damn Christmas tree, though. He took up his mug and drank half the remaining wine.

"Yeah, okay," said Billy.

"So, um, what have you been doing the last–eighteen years? Jeez, is it eighteen years?"

"I guess it is. Well, I went to college in Illinois. Northwestern. Studied engineering."

"And since then, what, you've been an engineer? What have you been up to?"

"Nothing, really." Billy looked like he didn't want to talk about it. That was all right. Douglas knew very well about not wanting to be pushed.

Rob came back from the kitchen and handed Billy a tall iced-tea glass. "Cheers," he said. He poured more wine into Douglas's mug.

"To friends less absent than before," said Rob. He and Billy clinked glasses and smiled at each other. Douglas wondered just how good friends the two were. "It's too damn quiet in here," Rob said. "Could drive a man crazy. Let's have some music, for god's sake!"

"Wait, Rob, come on–"

"You got any Christmas music?" Rob was squatting down by the short piles of CDs stacked in the corner behind the boombox Douglas used for his stereo. "No, no, no, no–your taste in music is still boring, pal, by the way–nothing Christmasy here at all. Where's your spirit, Dougy?"

"*Gee*, I'm sorry, Robby," Douglas said. "I didn't prepare properly for this party. Thoughtless of me."

"You ought to put this tree up," Billy said. He sounded worried. He rustled its branches, examining it. "It's getting dry already. Dying. And it's a fire hazard."

"No problem," said Rob. His bootheels made war on the floor as he went over to where his jacket lay on the floor. He pulled a blank-labeled cassette out of the inside breast pocket. "You wouldn't have seen this. It's the Christmas compilation album I waited all my life for. Sisters of Mercy doing 'Silver Bells'–really, I'm doing you such a favor." Three strides and the cassette was in the boombox. The first bars of "White Christmas" floated glumly across the room. It sounded like Lou Reed. Then it sounded very loudly like Lou Reed, as Rob cranked the volume all the way. "There's Christmas for you!"

"Let's put the tree up, okay?" said Billy. "Really, okay?"

"Dance first," said Rob. He grabbed Billy by the hand and swung him into the small clear space in the middle of the room. The creak-ing of the floor was just audible over the music booming through the apartment.

"Guys—"

"Okay, it's not the most danceable tune on the album," Rob shouted. "Next one works a lot better. Come on, we don't need to divide by partners for this, Dougy, get off your butt and enjoy yourself a little!"

Billy was dancing with his eyes shut, brow furrowed in concentration, head thrown forward, back. He was completely off the beat. His sneakers thudded more quietly than Rob's boots, but the floor was groaning.

"Great tune, but you really can't dance to it," Rob shouted. "Just a second!" He bent over the boombox. The music shut off as he hit Fast-Forward. Billy's solo shuffling was still loud, unaccompanied. There was no broomstick against his floor. She must have called the cops. Probably half the cops in the precinct were bearing down on him, pissed at having their Christmas disturbed.

Rob hit Play with a loud click and the boombox screamed with electric guitar. Douglas couldn't recognize the tune over the distortion and the riffs. "All *right!*" Rob shouted. He leapt into the air and crashed to the floor doing air-guitar. Billy increased his pace to a near-flamenco.

"Stop it!" Nothing changed. Douglas screamed, "*Stop* it!"

Rob stopped. Billy stopped. The music stopped.

"What the hell are you *doing* here? Are you just here to make what's left of my life hell?"

"Not us," said Rob.

"My neighbor hates me, you're going to get the cops called on me, maybe I'll be evicted, this could be my last goddamn Christmas and what are you *doing* to me?"

"Spending Christmas," Rob said.

"Jesus, don't you see it? I'm dying, you moron. You're spending your goddamn Christmas with a goddamn dead man."

"You?" Rob sounded amused.

"Did you ever hear of rest in peace? Would you get the hell out of here?"

"Everyone isn't here yet."

"You should put the tree up," Billy said. "You've got to trim off the bottom so it doesn't die so soon. I don't think you should wait any more."

"I don't give a damn about the tree. I hurt. I have nausea and I can't breathe right sometimes and you are pissing the hell out of me. Go away. Go away!"

"We have no place else, Douglas," said Rob. "For a so-called dead man you're not so swift on the uptake. You should at least give everyone else a chance to come by and have Christmas."

Billy went to the door and opened it. "I don't know these guys," he said.

"Jerry," said Rob. "Patrick. Carlos. George here?"

"Not yet," Carlos said. "He's a tough one."

"How are you doing, Douglas?" Jerry asked. The last time Douglas had seen him, he was skeletal, enmeshed in tubing, blotched with K/S. Five years ago. Now Jerry's thick hair was beginning to gray and there were more wrinkles around his eyes. He looked older.

Rob smirked. "Oh, he thinks he's dead already."

"There's a difference, Douglas. Trust me, you can tell," said Jerry.

"Do you have any of that wine?" Patrick asked Rob.

"In the kitchen," Rob said. "Help yourself. I'm turning the music back on." Electric guitar filled the room again, somewhat less deafeningly. Rob hadn't touched the boombox.

"Go away," Douglas said. "You're not real. Leave me alone. All of you." He sat heavily on his futon. It came to him that, beneath the wild improvisation, the tune was "I'll Be Home for Christmas". "Who the hell is playing that?"

"Hendrix," said Rob. He shrugged. "I waited all my life to hear Hendrix do Christmas. Had to wait for your life."

"Never understood why you were so into that guy," Jerry said.

"You're dead? Billy, *you're* dead?" Billy smiled faintly. "It?"

"Oh, no, that's the part I hate," Billy said. "I was a virgin. Wiped out by a semi truck. I was nineteen. I barely knew who I was yet; I was just figuring myself out. You're a lucky guy, Doug."

"Is that what this delirium is about?" He was furious. "My subconscious telling me where there's life, there's hope? Buck up, take your AZT, tomorrow there's a cure and true love is around the corner? Well, screw that. Tomorrow I could be in intensive care, and I never found true love, and I don't need a bunch of party animals from beyond the veil telling me pie in the sky!"

"Screw you," said Patrick, coming from the kitchen with a coffee mug of wine. "Who said this is anything about you, Douglas? What about us? Where the hell do we exist except in you? Our loving families? Give me a break. *You* go gentle, but if you're taking me with you I'm gonna fight, man."

Douglas blinked. His anger had spooled itself out in one burst and now he didn't know what to say.

"Hey," said Carlos. "We're the guests here, guys, be nice. Come on, Douglas, sit back down." His hand on Douglas's arm felt strong and real.

"If this is really your last Christmas, Douglas, how are you gonna spend it?" said Jerry. "Pretending for your neighbor's sake you're already dead?"

"Can we put the tree up?" Billy asked. "Let's put the tree up."

Douglas looked around at all of them. Hendrix faded into Sisters of Mercy. "It's really drying out, isn't it?" he said.

"Yeah, but it'll last a while longer if you get the bottom sawed off. You have a saw?"

"In the kitchen," Douglas said. "Bottom drawer next to the stove." Billy turned to get it. "Hey, Billy?"

"Yeah?"

"If—it happened—when you were nineteen, how come you look like my age?"

"It's 1993, Doug," Billy said. "How old should I get to be? I didn't come here to be nineteen forever."

Douglas nodded. "Right-hand side of the stove."

Officer Yi sighed as he climbed the stairs of the old Mission district building. He was too damn old to still be working Christmas Eves. His partner, Kelley, behind him, had heard about this building. "This dizzy old woman calls on this poor asshole all the time, Jim," he'd told Yi in the car. "Claims he's, I dunno, bowling with elephants up there. Every one noted as unsubstantiated when the cops got there. One night she called three times. I think she just hates his ass." Better than a domestic dispute, though. You never knew who might wave a gun in your face when you went to one of those.

He knocked loudly on the door. Get it over with and find out what the next call was. Finish the shift, then get about two hours of sleep before his kids woke him so they could tear into their stockings.

"George?" said a voice on the other side of the door. It opened. A very thin man in pajamas stood looking at him. He was pale, though there was color high in his cheeks. Another poor jerk with AIDS, for sure.

The man smiled crookedly and held up a teacup filled with wine. Behind him, in the corner of a small studio room, a scraggly, undecorated Christmas tree tilted at a precarious angle in its stand. A boombox hissed white noise.

"Oh. You're alive." He handed Yi the cup of wine. "Come in and help me get this tree straight, would you?"

Yi looked at his partner. *Looney-tunes,* Kelley mouthed.

Yi smiled. "What the hey, it's Christmas." It seemed like something to do. The three of them went into the apartment to fix the tree.

A Defense of
the Social Contracts

He flirted with all and he meant it with none, but Anli had been foolish enough to think he meant it with her.

That is the language of the bad old days. In these times we may be more fair than that to Anli and Derren. Derren was a registered nonmonogamist, than which little could be more clear. He was scrupulous enough to keep his preference license by the doorway of his privacy room, under his certificate of health, though this was not required. Who could ask more of Derren than that? Watch his movements, listen to his words in the context he has placed them in. Be rational.

Anli had recently withdrawn a registration of celibacy. It had stood two years and more, which is a long time for a citizen who has not taken celibacy as a life choice, but it is not unheard of.

Before her celibacy, she had offered three contracts of monogamy, two to men and one to a woman, which had not been accepted. Her friends suggested she brooded too much over the third rejection, by the second man, who took instead the offer of a group family. Anli had obliged their urgings and taken erotic rebalancing: through a combination of nano and of tailored drugs the doctors remapped her responses so she would not find men of his size, shape, coloring and vocal characteristics attractive. After the procedure she no longer woke in the middle of the night, breath-starved and sweat-drenched, the dream-touch of a blond, smooth, brown-eyed man fading too slowly to forget; she told her friends this so they would no longer worry.

She did not tell them she still brooded. She did not tell them of her unhealthy resentment at the loss of her fantasy.

In this light, we may say Anli was wise when she chose to register celibate. Or we may wonder why she did not go back to the doctors. Should not her decisions be judged by their results? These are not the dark old days, after all, when citizens approached each other as across a field of buried mines, whether blindfolded or not, still never able to entirely avoid danger when they touched. These are modern times, mapped and rational, and avoiding heartache is a simple matter of taking responsibility for oneself. The social contracts have been made clear. Who would argue otherwise?

Anli did not go back to the doctors, but she stayed celibate for two years, until she considered she was no longer brooding, or perhaps until brooding no longer made celibacy compelling. She reregistered as she had been before: open. After two weeks, from an open registration, she could switch again to whatever she desired: nonmonogamy, single or group partnership, or a dozen other, more arcane classifications and subclassifications.

Her friends held a party in her honor. Derren was at that party.

So were many men and women, nearly all registered open or nonmonogamous, a few registered to group families that were not full. Her friends had taken care to supply Anli with a full palette of human potential to celebrate her departure from celibacy. They gathered in the common hall of Anli's cooperative, making matches among each other or not as they chose, all polite enough to introduce themselves first to their guest of honor.

Derren himself did not arrive until near the end of the party. Had the party before worked out differently, he would not have stayed after it was over.

But for the first hour, two men from a group family flirted with her, and while she thought the first was funny and the second intriguing, she did not want to think about group families. And for the second hour she became engrossed in a discussion of jai-alai with another man who followed the same team she did, and while they exchanged access numbers and agreed to attend a game together soon, they also agreed to call each other Brother and Sister. And at the end of the third hour she nearly asked a wry and intense woman to stay after, but something familiar and carefully uninteresting about the woman's blonde hair and brown eyes and rich contralto voice changed her mind. Anli generally preferred men anyway, and did not demur when the woman, watching her, suddenly said she thought she might as well make an early night of it.

So by the fourth and last hour of her party, Anli sat in a corner of the hall trading word jokes with the remaining guests, reflecting that a change from celibacy to noncelibacy was more symbolic than predictive. It would be fair to Anli to say that she was not brooding on this, or did not see herself to be brooding: she laughed with her friends and argued which turn of phrase scored the most points in the game and had put aside any thought of exercising her new license that night.

"I'm sorry to be so late," said a tall man with dark hair and hazel eyes, a man Anli did not know. "Will someone tell me who our hostess is so I may apologize properly?" His soft voice teased and danced.

Anli stood and extended her hand. He stood looking at her for a long moment, then took her hand and kissed it, not dropping his eyes. He grinned, and said "With the beauty of the hostess and the circumstances of the party, it's my great luck she's still here to apologize to."

"I wouldn't abandon my guests before the party was over," Anli said lightly.

"The party is not over," he said. He had not released her hand.

They went to her privacy room, not across town to his, and made love under her certificate of openness rather than his of nonmonogamy, but he told her how he was registered beforehand. As a good citizen should. His nonmonogamous status, as she knew, meant he could not directly enter a partnership even if he wanted: he would have to pass through a two-month transition, registered open, first.

Derren's practice and experience stood him in good stead. Within an hour Anli had forgotten to even wonder if she was brooding.

Two citizens with an open registration may spend ten nights together without having to change their registration. After that, or before if things move quickly, they must discuss whether they will change their registrations to monogamy or provisional monogamy, or if they will list each other as nonexclusive partners, or start a group family.

These are all decisions Anli would have had to discuss with a lover who was open, as she was, but Derren's nonmonogamy gave him more latitude.

Perhaps it is ironic that Derren's nonmonogamy allowed Anli to see Derren more often without either of them reconsidering their registration. But we must note that most citizens understand that nonmonogamy is exactly what it says on the face of it. Most citizens do not have the difficulty facing straightforward reality, written on a certificate beside a bed, that Anli had. Society cannot be held to blame.

It is precisely because Anli did know that Derren was committed to being uncommitted that he could take her to his bed, or she take him to hers, so frequently. In that month, it was twenty times.

"Anli," he gasped as he shuddered into her. "Ah, you fit sweetly. No other the same."

Anli shuddered herself, a shudder of warmth and happiness, and rolled to his side. "No other?" she teased. "Of your hundred women?"

"Not a hundred," he said, and chuckled, "not this year, but if it were a hundred, none of them like you."

How did Anli hear these words? Was she bearing in mind the social contracts, as every schoolchild knows to? Should we offer her sympathy for remembering those words only, and not what he had said three nights before? "Ah, Anli, you're a change from any other woman I know," he'd said. "How nice to be surprised again after all these years. If you change your registration again, love, you should think about registering as I have. There's nothing like the thrill of discovery."

She may have remembered part of that, but not the parts we would note. She may have placed undue weight on "love". Understanding this does not mean approving this. The very fact she teased him about a hundred women must mean she herself understood he was, indeed, exactly as the social contract presented him.

In that month Derren slept twenty times with Anli, and a dozen or more times with old friends, most of them also nonmonogamous, and a few new friends, some nonmonogamous and some open. Derren was in the higher percentiles for sexual activity, as are many who register nonmonogamous. You will assume he mentioned some of this other activity to Anli; you will assume correctly. He only mentioned it a few times, but why should he have mentioned it more?

Anli slept twice with other men, one of whom irked her by too soon mentioning that he was looking for a partnership, and one of whom had skills she thought compared unfavorably to Derren's. She contacted Derren and was with him an hour after the second man left.

"We should keep doing this," she said after Derren had confirmed her judgment.

"I'll have to stop for at least ten minutes, love," he joked, running the back of his hand gently down her sweat-dampened side.

She smiled back at him. "I mean that we should keep seeing each other," she said.

"I'll happily keep seeing you, no fear. Not as often as we have been. I've been neglecting some of my other friends too much, they tell me."

Anli paused. "I was thinking of a contract," she said.

Derren sat up. Of course this would be a surprise to him. "Anli, love, I'm nonmonogamous."

"You could reregister."

"After first reregistering open, for two months, before I would be allowed to take a contract—and why would I? I'm nonmonogamous, Anli, I've been nonmonogamous for twelve years. You can see the dates on my certificate. You know who I am."

"You like me, you like being with me," Anli said. "You could be happy in a partnership with me."

"I like many people, Anli," said Derren. He was frowning, now. He pulled the sheet up past his waist.

"But you don't need them."

"I want them all, yes," Derren said. He spoke slowly, watching her. "I want many women, but I don't need any one of them. I am not monogamous. I do not need any one of you."

Did he see Anli flinch? He did.

"We have, perhaps, seen too much of each other, love," he said. "You were open. I thought perhaps open to my way of living. Perhaps I misjudged. I've never slept with someone who had been so long celibate before. Does that make a difference? Have you seen anyone other than me?"

"Several people," Anli said, exaggerating, and then she said, "I think you're right about my registration. I'll think about it. I'll call you." She dressed then, and left.

Derren's adherence to responsibility cannot be denied. Anli, however—

Anli appeared at Derren's doorway three days later with a piece of paper in her hand. She glanced only once at the woman sitting up in Derren's bed, peering curiously around him at her, then said "I decided you have the best idea. I've changed my registration."

He looked at the paper. It read Nonmonogamous. He looked at her.

"So, I'll give you a call sometime, all right?" Anli said.

"All right. I have company—"

"I won't keep you." She left his building and went back to her own. She took her certificate off the wall and carefully smoothed the forged one over it. She waited to see if she would hear from Derren.

If any of you is vulnerable to backwards thinking, you may say this was a small crime. But it is well said that the smallest breach in the social contracts leads to dangerous rifts: plunging, deadly chasms of conflict and misunderstanding. Insanity. It is not for nothing that our forebears set up our system of social contracts. Eternal vigilance is the price of sociability.

Learn from Anli's errors.

When Derren did not call for several days, Anli contacted him, and, keeping her voice as casual as she could, arranged for him to come to her privacy room.

She found her thoughts strangely divided while he was there. She was glad to see him, and triumphant at the success of her fraud. (Derren did not even glance at the false certificate on her wall. Who would falsify a certificate?)

And yet, as she kissed him and he stroked her hips and breathed into her ear, she was tormented by the thought that he would as soon be with the redheaded woman she had seen in his bed as with her. She had conceived, so she thought, a true passion for him, while to him she was an interchangeable partner, one among many.

She found this thought unbearable.

It was, she thought, even as she moved in complex rhythms with the man, worse than being rejected for partnership by someone registered open. It was infinitely worse, because he did not even look at her as the material for a partnership.

This, though Derren was nonmonogamous from the start of things.

We see that, so soon after her first crime, Anli had begun to slip into what we can only call insanity. Backwards-thinking people might call it jealousy, or insecurity, or even love, but we know there is no place for love that is not law abiding. And we can see this from Anli's desperate actions to follow.

She now saw Derren only every week or two. Between times, she thought about little but the next time she would see him. When they spent an hour together, it seemed to her Derren was reserved, much more cautious in his dealings with her than he had been before. She brooded.

She brooded, and she did not take this as a sign to change her ways: instead, she plotted how to change Derren's ways. This is a violation of all the principles of the social contracts. The social contracts were designed to help Anli and all citizens easily find those others who could suit their needs, so they would not violate the rights of other citizens by trying to change them.

Anli had had failures, but who of us has not? Her error was in brooding. Her error was in turning criminal against the principles of social contracts. Her error was in not keeping faith with the system.

Anli tried arranging surprises of dress, food or activity with Derren; she tried reading the latest poems and being witty; she tried seven fashions of styling her hair and coloring her eyes. She stuck to her lie of nonmonogamy but slept only with Derren, when she could.

Which was not often.

Although she had broken the contracts and broken her word, giving a fellow citizen no understanding of her desires or intentions, Derren pulled back. We may look at it as though he saw her true self under the false, a rough skin under the soft, her real certificate under the forgery.

Which of course he could not. No citizen could be prepared for such dissembly. Perhaps we should blame the doctors Anli went to two years before, that they did not find her flaw. Or perhaps we can still only blame her, who knew her own flaw and did not strive to have it removed.

But, as he pulled back, whatever ancient instinct guiding him, Anli grew more desperate, and as she grew more desperate, more criminal.

Each citizen devotes twenty hours a week to her work (Anli had a technical position with the weather service, tracking which storms were likely and which necessary, and determining when to alter their patterns), and ten to social services, which at this time she spent removing old broadsheets and flyers from walls and kiosks. Neither occupation, we can see, afforded her much interaction with her fellow citizens. Her weather analysis she conducted alone, in her own privacy room; the flyer-removal was a simple task that took her out in public, but did not require her to as much as speak to anyone. It also gave her every opportunity to brood, which she did, even in good sunlight and surrounded by adjusted, normal people.

It is not good for someone with retrogressive tendencies to shun societal contact, but just as she did in her work, she stayed to herself in her free hours.

Somewhere in the midst of this unhealthy solitude she conceived her desperate plan.

In this one area the city might be held accountable. There obviously were insufficient safeguards on the personal files of its citizens. Yet there is no record that anyone before had attempted to alter the parts of those files Anli now compromised. Perhaps some had tried before and failed. Perhaps she found an untapped genius within herself.

Through trickery, finesse and deceit she found a way to change the files, from her own home workstation. Within a week of her determination to make it so, Derren's registration was changed to open, backdated six weeks.

The certificate on his wall was the same as ever. Anli could see it on the occasions she was there, as she smiled at him, lying to him by the very way she carried herself, breaking the social contracts.

Only twice she saw him in the next two weeks, but during them she relaxed and smiled. Their sex was much better, relaxed, as, perhaps, Derren sensed the brooding cloud she had carried was gone. He mentioned something about taking a day to visit the summer fair with her.

"That would be perfect," said Anli. The fair was two days after two weeks after she had altered his records.

We are all rightly proud of our famous summer fair, that fabulous gathering of jugglers, clowns, acrobats, holo-illusionists, personality readers, contests and music. A hundred different foods are flash-grown in tanks of colorful fluids, cooked and served in the open air.

Nearly the whole city attends at least a full day, and others come from thousands of miles away to see it.

Anli met Derren at a roast-apple stand and offered him one. They strolled arm in arm down the street. Derren pointed out a group of acrobats tumbling up and down invisible rappelling lines along a building's side. Two leapt unexpectedly ten meters through empty air to the next building over, making them gasp and laugh. Anli pulled him to a stand where a musical trio she liked, horn, viola and a gene-modified canary controlled by a trainer, was playing. They ate again, chopped potatoes with herbs and sausage.

And, for an hour, Anli thought she would not do what she had planned to do. She took Derren's arm, leaned against his side, and drifted through the crowds feeling perfectly right in the world. She was, as we understand, deluding herself. She allowed herself to feel Derren's falsified social contract status was his true one, that he was open to a partnership; but the truth could not be plastered over.

For Derren removed her arm from his and said "Wait, just a moment, please?" And went over to a tall, fair woman pouring cider at a booth; Anli could hear them laughing as old friends do, and hear them set a date for later in the week. Her fingers stiffened, clenched, marked her palms with her nails. She did not notice. She watched Derren and the tall woman, her breath painful in the back of her throat.

She stood back. She pulled the device from her belt that linked her up to her systems at home, and to the citywide systems. She issued an instruction.

The results of further planning, deceit and trickery fell into place.

When Derren returned, Anli said "I'm tired of walking. Could we go back to my place now?"

"I'd rather see more of the fair," Derren said. "There's a pantomime I want to watch that begins in less than an hour."

"I don't feel well. Please help me home."

Anli pulled Derren away, between the stilts of performers who moved slowly through the crowd, dipping as low as three meters and souring as high as ten on the telescoping stilts; red satin capes rippled in the breeze high over the pair's heads, meter-wide butterflies with wings patterned to match the capes flying evanescently among them.

"Anli, love," Derren was saying, as she twisted them quickly toward her building through waves of smiling people moving the other direction, "Anli, I think we should talk. You don't really seem the sort of person suited to nonmonogamy. You say you've been see- ing other people, but no one I know has seen you with anyone else for months." So, we can see that Derren was not himself a fool. He understood the social contracts, and had some intuition of Anli's resistance to them. Could he have expected the lengths to which she would go? No one could have.

Anli did not reply. She quickened her pace, so that Derren had to lengthen his stride to keep up. He said, "You're a special woman and our time has been sweet, but perhaps you should register as open again, and find someone who wants a partnership, Anli." They reached her building and Anli signaled the door to open. "Love, I'll see you to your room, but then I think I should go."

Anli nodded impatiently. The door opened; they were inside. She shut it.

"Are you all right now? I should leave."

"You have to see something."

Derren frowned as Anli pulled at the mail drawer by her work- station. She removed an envelope and took two sheets of paper from it. Her eye was bright, her cheeks flushed. She showed them to him.

"I don't need a partnership. I have one."

Derren looked at the papers. They were not simple forgeries, like the certificate of nonmonogamy Anli had fooled him with earlier, the one he had never thought to examine skeptically. They were freshly delivered from the city's record-keeping center itself, when Anli had triggered her mad plan from the fair. They were as legal and legiti- mate as any contracts in the city—if we can say that anything is legit- imate with deliberate error and deceit at its base.

"What is this?"

"We have a partnership," Anli said, and the calm satisfaction in her voice could only be called quite mad.

Imagine what Derren felt then. Imagine yourself, if the founda- tions on which you had built your life were with no warning perverted against you: if your parent or co-parent called you stranger; if you came home and found your room a factory filled with silk-spinning vats instead of your own comfortable furniture and belongings, and the building manager insisted it was ever so; if you found yourself arrested for the crime of performing the ordinary job you had worked for three years.

So must Derren have felt, and we cannot be surprised that he found no words at first, that his knees weakened so he must sit dizzily on the chair Anli pushed up behind him.

"We do not," he finally said. "That is madness."

"I have the certificates. I can show you the city records," she said, stepping past him to her workstation. Derren shook his head in stunned disbelief at what she showed him.

He said it was not true, and Anli made him call up the records from his own link. He said he had not so registered, and she smiled. He said the city records must have misfunctioned somehow, and she reminded him such had not happened in thirty years. He said he would reregister, and she asked if he had forgotten the minimum partnership term was three months.

He said he was not her partner.

Anli said, "You are."

He stood, with a near violence rarely seen in a modern citizen, staring at her wildly. Then he slumped back into the chair and pulled at his hair. "I don't understand, I don't understand."

"I applied and it went through. You must have applied as well."

"I couldn't have! I'm nonmonogamous! I always have been!"

"That's not what the city said," Anli said, her voice clear and innocent.

"You were registered nonmonogamous!"

"I changed my registration back two months ago. Didn't I tell you? I thought I'd told you." She gestured at the wall, where her certificate hung. The forged paper had been removed from over her true certificate, but now her true certificate was a forgery as well: its beginning date altered to two months, two days before.

"It makes no sense," he said, moaning, "no sense."

She paused. "We're in a partnership now. Three months, that's all. Such a little time. Why not try it, Derren?"

"I will live my life as I always have," he said. The anger in his voice would have caused any normal person to step back. Anli stepped forward and brushed slack hair from his forehead with the edge of her hand.

"You will not," she said. "You cannot."

He got up and left then without another word. We might have expected Anli would have locked her door against his exit, but she had not. She watched him leave, and sat in the chair he had unwillingly warmed, and waited. In a while she ordered some food to her door; in a while she did a little work, approving a hurricane's deflection away from the coast. She hummed sometimes to herself. She did not brood. She waited.

The madness was ripe. It was full.

The next day Derren returned. His breath was short and his eye wild, but he kept his voice nearly low. "They have all been informed. Every woman I know. They all received official notice that I am partnered. They all congratulated me!"

"They must be polite and gracious women," Anli said. "I'm sure they're very happy for you."

"They will not receive me!"

"Of course not," said Anli. "It's the social contract."

"How can I live my life?" he cried. "I am not made for celibacy!"

"I am here, my partner."

For the first time he looked at her with something like hatred. For a normal citizen to feel hatred, he must have been driven to an extreme. Anli met his glare and did not flinch.

"It will not be," he said, and left again.

Anli took two hours away from home to perform her social duties. She slid through the crowds of the fair with a sprayer of defixative, examining kiosks for outdated notices, spraying them and peeling them off. She smiled; she fairly glowed with satisfaction. Other citizens caught her eye and smiled back. Some laughing clowns grabbed her hands and pulled them into their troupe; she danced with them down the street on a platform atop a giant slow-moving ball that swirled with colors in time to the dance. She dismounted and went back to work, humming in counterpoint to the strains of the street musicians. She rolled up the old flyers, dropped them into a recycling bin, and returned to her home.

Early the next night Derren returned. "You did something," he accused.

"I? I agreed to a partnership with you," she said. "You're lucky I'm an understanding woman. Another might have notified the city that you are derelict in your duties."

Derren made a wordless noise and fled. He did not come back that night, or the night after. Anli did her work and watched the days go by.

After a week and some days, she went to his room. She signaled the door and it let her in. "You!" said Derren, sitting up groggily, one person in a bed made for two. "How did—"

"We are partnered," said Anli. "The city knows that. Your building knows that. I have entry here."

A sob broke from Derren.

"I understand," she said. "You've been alone. That's hard for you. I am your partner: I am here."

"No," said Derren.

She sat on the bed beside him. "You shouldn't have to feel like this," she said. She was wearing a scent he had given her.

"No." He pulled away.

She pulled her legs up onto the bed and removed her light evening jacket. Under it she wore a thin, sheer camisole. "Yes," she said.

Derren closed his eyes and shuddered. We must understand what Anli did, what we noted earlier: as most citizens who choose lifelong nonmonogamy, Derren was in the highest percentiles for sexual need. He had not been two weeks without a bedmate since he was fifteen. We can only speculate on the pressures within him, in a position the social contracts should never have allowed, unwilling to submit to a lie made real in the city records about his very nature. But a man battered by abstinence. "No."

Anli brushed a finger, feather soft, around his ear, and the fingertips of her other hand up his opposite thigh, in a manner he had always moaned to feel. He moaned now, in agony more than pleasure.

"No—"

She kissed him on the jawline. He trembled. Tears rolled from his eyes.

"No," he said, a last time.

When he woke in the morning she was asleep, curled beside him smiling, both her arms wrapped around his, her leg across his leg.

We must find sympathy for Derren. The madness had not been his. He had not first cracked and then shattered the social contracts to serve his own selfish ends: Anli had shattered those, and his life, his public and thus his private self, with them.

What happened was appalling, then, but it stemmed naturally from Anli's crimes, and not from Derren himself.

Still, the city might not have found out for days, not until far too late, if Derren had not been so broken, so driven to his own reflective madness, moon to Anli's sun, that he went out wildly searching the fair until he found a woman from a distant city who he had met, once, years past, one who would not have received notice of his changed status. He stayed with her at her hostel; only the next morning did she idly link up to her host city's records to check on his status. He had not said if he was still nonmonogamous, and she herself, open to partnership, looked to see if he now was.

She notified the authorities, of course. They came to arrest Derren before he woke.

Someone backwards-thinking might call him a broken man, but he was performing his duty as a citizen by telling the city representatives everything that had happened. An ambulance was immediately dispatched to his privacy room, an override ordered for the lock on his door.

They found Anli on the floor beside the bed, neck broken, but still breathing.

Still smiling.

It was a simple matter to repair her broken body, grow nerves back to touch nerves, mend a shattered vertebra. Within days this was done.

Her madness was another matter. The city gives each citizen every opportunity to reconcile with its principles. While her record of mental health was examined, while her erotic remapping studied to see if errors had been made, Anli appeared before a hearing of the city elders. They listened as she put her words on record, words that would become part of her file.

"There can be no contract to make everyone happy," she said. "There are no rules for love. You're fools, all of you, all of us for thinking we can sort everyone by some kind of emotional taxonomy. Do you think you can order everyone to lie down neatly in rows for you?"

She stood and shook her fist. She thought herself heroic and defiant at this moment. We can only picture her thin arm waving, her strained voice spouting irrationalities.

"If my heart is broken, it is mine to be broken. If I am a fool, there can be no sane law against it."

But how may the insane speak of sanity? How may the criminal claim she damages no one but herself?

"However you made it my duty to be happy, you could not compel it from me. However many cozy boxes you designed for me, I could not fit into one. Is this my fault? Yours? Nature's? I call on the people to erase their registrations. Walk into chaos as human beings, not social components! Stumble blindly among your fellow blind men and women! Collide, confuse, hurt each other. You're fooling yourselves if you think everyone can herd their feelings like domestic animals. Why try? Why submit? Why–"

The council looked silently down at her.

"Revolt!" Anli said, but her voice was cracked, and she let them take her away.

No citizen may be treated against her will. Ours is a society of freedom and democracy. Derren's treatment was simple–his madness only temporary and reactive–and he was released to live a life as adjusted as it had been before. At his request, he forgot Anli entirely.

Anli had the stubbornness of true madness. But madness will burn itself out after enough years of protective custody; if it doesn't, society is patient. The social contracts will out, in the end.

So finally, with caring help, Anli was erotically rebalanced, socially adjusted, and sent back into society.

Her home had been held empty for her return by the generosity of the city. Her friends welcomed her with open arms, and a party as warm as the one that had marked the beginning of her criminal path. A new post was created for her at the weather bureau, awaiting only the completion of one small task which she happily completed for society's sake.

Learn from her errors: her story is published herewith as a caution to all citizens. Had she sought help when she showed the signs of early madness, the uncontrolled brooding, the first small crimes, society would have been spared much labor, Anli much pain.

Learn from her errors: all her mad rebellion bought was that pain.

Learn from her errors: in the design of the social contracts, in our agreement to them, are the tools to keep us all on a calm and healthy path. Society is perfectable: it is a simple matter of codifying it to meet every human need.

If society is perfectable, it is the responsibility of the individual to be perfectable. It would be madness to think madness cannot be made obsolete, defeatism to think citizens might continue to deny themselves the proferred means to be calm and fulfilled. It would be the worst sort of defeatism to deny the perfectibility of humankind.

Who could disagree?

This document sworn before the Council of City Elders and signed by the reportant, Anli Vennera: citizen.

Jones and the Stray

Jones blew hard to see how far out her breath would fog. Pretty far. It seemed to her it must be possible–if the wind was still and there was the same amount of moisture in the air–to guess the temperature by the length of breath cloud you could blow. If you'd filled your lungs with the same amount of air and blew just as hard.

Well, that was an awful lot of ifs. Maybe not.

When you were in Alaska in the winter, you always knew it was cold, anyway, and you'd better never let yourself forget it if you wanted to stay alive.

She was rattling at the doorknob of her warehouse. Jones called it her warehouse; whoever's warehouse it actually was wasn't using it for anything. It was a small, wind-leaky, smelly building, thrown together years ago out of corrugated steel.

What was important was that no one had ever turned off the electricity, and that the lock would give if you jiggled it just right. Of course she didn't have the key.

"Come on, door," Jones said, making two more puffs of frosty breath that drifted back past her ear.

The doorknob felt cold even through the glove of her heatsuit. The suit's charge was wearing down. She'd taken off the big knit glove she usually wore over the thin heatsuit glove, and was holding it in the other big knit glove. She wore lots of layers of wool and polyester over the suit, to hold in heat and save the charge. And to make her look bigger, and more anonymous.

She had brought the heatsuit with her from Seattle, with all the money she had been able to scrounge in a hurry. That was all she had, when she left. Her name she acquired a day or two later. She made it up on the long bus trip north, right after she cut her hair short and shaggy in a diner restroom. "Jones." If you said it fast and gruff no one might notice exactly who was under all those clothes, especially if you were tall for your age.

Not if you didn't give them too much time to look at you.

"Come on!" she whispered urgently, and the lock slipped, the door opened.

She gave one quick glance behind her and ducked inside.

It was even darker here than it was outside. A little bit of moonlight came in through the cracks in the wall panels. Jones found the light switch. She crossed her fingers, hoping the lights would come on. They did. There was still electricity.

It was funny how you never noticed how tight your shoulders were until they relaxed. Jones turned the lights off again quickly, so that no one would see them, and hurried to the far corner of the warehouse. She felt with her hand for the electrical outlet. With her other hand she took the heavy square transformer from one of her many pockets. She plugged the little lead from the transformer into the suit's connector under her armpit. She plugged the big lead into the electrical outlet in the concrete floor.

She lay back awkwardly against the crinkled wall. The heatsuit wasn't really designed to be recharged while you were still wearing it. You were supposed to be indoors someplace warm, letting it charge back up overnight on a table somewhere while you were in a nice soft bed under all the covers.

Jones reached inside her layers of clothes to a big pocket and found dinner, a plastic bag from inside a cereal box, half full of puffed corn. She leaned on her left elbow and started eating it with her right hand. The crunch of the cereal was loud and satisfying. She settled in and let her gaze drift across the blackness.

A pair of eyes was looking at her from the near corner of the warehouse.

Jones gasped before she could stop it and clutched her cereal bag close. She drew herself up against the wall as far as she could without unplugging herself, and felt inside her pockets for the long steel wrench she carried there.

"Who's there?" she said loudly in her deepest, gruffest growl.

Silence for a moment.

"Bad," came a thin little voice. "Bad run bad boy hungry food stay away food."

"What?" said Jones, forgetting for a moment in her surprise to use her Jones-voice. She found the wrench.

"Bad," the voice said again. "Bad boy dangerous stay away bite bad food hungry food please."

It didn't sound like a man's voice or a woman's voice or a kid's voice. It sounded like a computer, like the computer in class when she still went to school, or the computer her friend Cary used to play games on. Under the voice she could hear the wet sound of heavy breathing.

The eyes were big and round, with a greenish blue glow in the tiny glint of moonlight. They blinked and stared at her.

Jones thought he must have been in there much longer than her, and his eyes would be better adjusted; but no one could see very well in here. She yanked the plug from her suit, dropped her food, and stood with the wrench held high, trying to look big in all her clothes.

"Leave now and there won't be trouble!" she cried in her best mean man's voice.

He barked. Jones almost dropped the wrench.

"Go away go away bad bite bad boy bad dog mean bite go," said the thin computer voice.

"Dog?" said Jones. She squinted, and could barely make out its shaggy gray shape. Lowering the wrench, but holding it tightly, she took a step forward.

The dog whined, and at the same time the voice said "Bad go scared go bad bad bad bite food please scared." It scrunched back as far as it could go in the corner, whimpering.

"Poor dog," Jones said. "Poor thing, I won't hurt you."

Now she could make out its voder collar. She'd seen rich people walking poodles that were wearing those. The collars had little computers in them that could translate a dog's brain waves into words. It took a lot of training for dogs to use them, and they were expensive. This dog seemed, in the gloom, as scruffy and scared as any stray she'd ever seen, but it must have a rich owner, to afford both the collar and the genetic work that improved its verbal skills so it could use it. She took another slow step forward.

The dog whimpered again. It said, through the collar, "Back bad mean dog bite bite back." Then it moaned and said "Scared hungry scared."

"It's okay," she said gently. She walked backward, feeling for the cereal bag with her foot. She put the wrench on the floor and took a handful of cereal, holding it out in front of her. "See? Here's some food. It's okay."

The dog was silent, but it stared at her hand.

Jones crouched down, tiptoeing on her haunches to the dog, with the food held out. Now she was right in front of it.

The dog was so still it could have been a stuffed animal. Its eyes looked up from the food to her face. "It's okay," she said, almost whispering. "It's okay. I'm a friend. It's okay."

The dog didn't take its eyes off hers, but then its muzzle was in her hand, its breath warm and moist through the mesh of her heat-suit glove. It licked and ate up the cereal with delicate little movements of its mouth, staring at her.

"See? It's okay. I'm a friend." She reached out to touch its head and the dog ducked its head away. Jones felt hurt. Then she thought it must still be scared. "It's okay," she said again. She dug through her pockets and found some pretzels, and put them on the floor in front of the dog. "You can have whatever you want."

The dog ate the pretzels. She watched. She could see it better, now that she was close and her eyes had adjusted. It was one of those pretty white dogs. She knew their name: a Samoyed. When they were puppies they looked like toys, with their black button eyes and their fluffy fur and tails. This one was not a little puppy, but it was not full grown, and its fur was dingy and matted with dirt.

"I'm Jones," she said to the dog. "Jones." She patted her chest.

The dog finished eating. It looked at her again. "Ohnz," it said. "Jones."

"Gohnz. Ohnz. Bones."

Jones laughed. "Not bones. Jones."

"Shones. Jones."

"Jones. Good, yes, Jones."

Carefully, Jones reached out and stroked its head. The dog let her do it. Encouraged, she rubbed its ear and neck. She couldn't remember the last time she'd petted a dog. But there weren't a lot of nice things she remembered—and plenty of things she didn't intend to remember—from before she'd left Seattle.

The dog yelped. She pulled back her hand. "What's wrong?" There was something sticky on her glove. She looked at it. "You're bleeding!"

"Hurt run away bad boy hurt," the dog said. She reached to see where the blood was. The dog cringed away.

"It's okay," Jones said. "I'm your friend. I want to see where you're hurt."

She put her hand on its neck and pulled the dog gently around to look at its other side. It whimpered softly, and its collar said "Hurt bad no please," but it let her do it.

A piece of the dog's skin hung, torn and wet-looking, from its flank. Jones's throat felt funny when she saw it: she had to swallow, hard. She made herself look. It was roughly the shape of a triangle, torn from the top, hanging down at the bottom. The flank where the skin had torn off was raw and unpleasant to see.

"What happened?" she asked the dog. "How did you do this? How did you hurt yourself?"

"Hurt," the dog said. It had stopped whimpering, and it looked at her as though it expected something. "Hurt."

"How did you hurt yourself?" she asked again.

"Run away bad dog," it said. "Run away bad master. Hide. Hide inside catch hurt catch pull hurt."

"Catch what? Hurt where?"

The dog looked along the wall of the warehouse toward the door. She looked where it was looking, and could see, just a few feet away, that a join where two sheets of steel had been welded together had come loose. The tear in the wall was only a few inches wide. The dog must have forced its way in through it.

"Did you hurt yourself coming through that hole?" She pointed. "That hole? That hole hurt you?"

"Yes hurt hide inside hide run away yes."

"You poor thing," Jones said again. She hugged it around the neck, hearing its breath in her ear. "Poor dog, why are you hiding?"

"Hide."

"Why?"

"Bad dog run away hide."

"I don't think you're a bad dog," Jones said. When the dog heard "bad dog" it cringed. "No no," she said. "Good dog. You're a good dog. Why did you run away?"

"Hit bad dog hit shout hit run away run away," the dog said.

"Did your master hit you?" Jones asked, feeling her cheeks burn with outrage. Just thinking of it made her want to hit someone back, though she'd promised herself she would never do that.

"Hit bad dog," it said.

"Bad master," Jones said. Her eyes stung.

"Bad master," said the dog.

She made herself calm down. She didn't want to upset the dog. She petted it quietly for a while. "We have to get you fixed," she said. She winced. "Not fixed fixed, I mean we have to get your wound fixed."

"Fix," said the dog. "Help."

"I don't know how to get you help," Jones said. She remembered a veterinary clinic a little to the side of town. How could she just go in there with a runaway dog–her, a runaway herself? They wouldn't be open until morning anyway.

"Jones fix," said the dog.

"Oh, no," Jones said. "I can't fix it." Runaway kids were sent home. Her face was probably on milk cartons. They could look inside their databanks and figure out where to send her back. Freezing in a shed would be better than that.

"Jones fix."

"Sweetie, I don't know how to, I don't have medicine and tools, I can't do it, honey–what is your name?"

The dog was quiet.

"Your name?" Jones said, very clearly.

"Name no. Master shout name bad bad name no. Name bad."

That was almost funny. "You and me, we've got a lot in common. Should I give you a name? Do you want to pick a name?"

The dog looked confused. "Jones fix."

"Okay," Jones said. "Um. Okay. Um. How about Diogenes? He went away from home to find an honest man. I read it in a book about old Greek philosophers. They didn't say if he ever found one." The dog put its head in her lap. "Diogenes?" She said it slowly and carefully: Dye Ah John Eez.

The dog tried the name. "Ah geez."

"Ah-geez," Jones agreed. It wasn't the dumbest name she'd ever heard, and the dog was the only one in the world who had it.

"Cold," said Ah-geez. "Hurt cold." The computer voice was calm and ordinary, every word coming out the same. But the dog was beginning to tremble.

"Oh lord," said Jones. "I can't do anything until morning. What if you've got infected? I think if you're sick you have to be specially careful to stay warm." The dog's pelt looked warm, but the place it was torn looked fragile and dangerous. With her heatsuit still warm, covering her up from her toes to most of her face, she hadn't thought how painful the freezing air would be on the wound. "Okay," she said. "Okay."

She took off all her many layers of clothes, the biggest on the outside and the smallest on the inside. She unzipped her heatsuit. The cold air hit her like a fist. "Oh my pete's sake geez!" she said. She hurried back into all her other clothes. It was cold, without the heatsuit. She wondered if she could get through a night that cold.

"Here you go," she said. "You have to help me get this over you."

Ah-geez looked uncomprehending, but when she lifted the dog up to try to get its back legs into the legs of the suit, it shifted itself around to help. She pulled the suit up slowly. When she got to the torn part, she winced and put the torn skin back carefully in place, figuring it had to be less dirty than the inside of her suit. Ah-geez yelped when she touched the wounded part, then was still, breathing hard.

Jones got the front legs into the heatsuit's arms. She left the suit's hood and mask down, since they wouldn't fit over a dog's face. It all made a lumpy weird shape, a lumpy shape she was perhaps the first person ever to discover. Dog inside heatsuit.

"Better?" she asked.

"No cold," Ah-geez said.

"Good," she said.

"Good Jones Jones good," the dog said.

"You're welcome," she said. "Now we wait until morning and then I'll think of something."

Shivering, she huddled up against the dog's unwounded side, and waited for the next dark morning. The dog slept, kicking softly, as dogs do, when it dreamed.

Jones fought to stay awake. She kept watch all night, just like hundreds of nights in Seattle, worrying her way into the next day.

The sun didn't come up properly in Alaska in the winter. It clung to the horizon, like sunrise all day. So the streetlights were on and it still felt like night when Jones struggled toward the vet clinic, arms full of lumpy dog.

She wished the streetlights would just short out, make everything as dark as could be. She felt obvious and exposed, everything she had run north not to be.

Mostly she felt exhausted. She could carry Ah-geez, but the dog felt heavier with every step she took. She couldn't shift her arms around without worrying about hurting the torn part of its flank.

She had turned the suit off before leaving the shed, but the dog still felt hot, very hot, too hot. That was what had made up her mind. Ah-geez was sick. There had to be an infection for the dog to be that hot, so much hotter than when she had first found it.

A woman was unlocking the door of the clinic when Jones staggered up. She turned and saw Jones and her bundle. "Good morning," she said, as though a skinny shortish person in a lot of clothes, carrying a misshapen bulk of heatsuit with a dog's head panting out of it, was a sight she saw every day.

"Hi," said Jones, and was terrified. She forced her nerves down. "Are you the animal doctor?"

"I am," said the woman. "Doctor Kozlowski. Is that your dog?"

"No," said Jones. "Yes. I mean." She'd had something all planned out to say, something to maybe throw them off and keep them from looking for her before she could be on a bus and going somewhere else. But it all fell out of her mind. Months of not talking to anyone, silently spending her last dollars on food to supplement what she could scavenge, ducking through the streets trying to look dangerous the rest of the time. She'd forgotten how to talk to people. "He's hurt, I think he's sick too."

"You'd better come inside," Dr. Kozlowski said. Jones found herself inside and in a bright little examining room in what seemed like four or five steps. She kept her eye on the door.

"What's your name?" the veterinarian asked the dog, noting the voder collar. She was stripping off the suit with sure, efficient hands.

The dog lay panting and didn't answer. "Ah-geez," Jones said.
The vet looked surprised. "How do you spell that?"

"I haven't any idea," Jones said. She stood by the examining-room door, calculating the fastest way out of the building.

"He's not your dog, is he? Did you find him?"

Jones wouldn't give her any clues. She shoved her hands in her pockets and waited, glancing at the door.

"You did a good job, keeping him warm. This must hurt him, here." Dr. Kozlowski examined the wound with gentle fingers. "I'll give him a shot of antibiotic, and clean this up, and then we should be able to sew it back where it belongs." She shook her head, looking at the damage. "I'll need to find his owner."

Jones had been waiting for a moment when the vet was distracted, to make her dash, but when she heard this she cried "No!"

The vet frowned. "No?" Her fingers moved across Ah-geez's dirty fur, pulling it this way and that like an outfielder looking for a softball in tall grass. "Ah. This dog has been hit," she said to herself. "There, there. Another scar there. Oh yes. Creep."

"You'll take care of him?" Jones asked. Oh please, she thought. Don't send him back.

"This dog has been hit, and I don't think he's been fed enough. And he's still a puppy. No, I don't think I'll be sending him back where he came from," Dr. Kozlowski said. "We'll take care of him." She was preparing a needle now.

"I can't pay you," Jones said.

"Don't worry about that," said the vet. "I'm on the animal-protection board. I'm their consulting veterinarian. We do that. You did a good thing, bringing Ah-geez–Ah-geez?–here."

"Um. Thanks." The vet was putting the needle under the dog's skin; Ah-geez twitched. Jones inched toward the chair over which the vet had draped her heatsuit.

"Jones help," said the dog in its thin voder voice. "Jones hurt help." Jones was stealthily lifting her suit from the chair. She froze.

"Your friend?" the woman said. "Yes, she helped you."

"Jones," the computer voice said insistently. "Jones Jones Jones hurt Jones hurt. Jones hurt help cry. Bad master hit Jones Jones asleep cry. Cry asleep cry bad master."

She had not! Jones thought, flushing. She'd been awake all night, watching over Ah-geez. She thought. Anyway, maybe she had night-mares about—all that. A long time ago. But she didn't cry in her sleep, not ever, not asleep or awake. She couldn't afford to let anyone know what the tears were about.

Not even a dog. But she must have fallen asleep from exhaustion without realizing it, so exhausted she talked in her sleep. The vet would figure out she was a runaway, and then—

The door was very far away. She had to get out before everything fell apart.

The vet was cleaning the wound, and she didn't look at Jones. She said, in the same calm voice she'd talked about antibiotics and stitches, "Sometimes when a dog gets hit enough, he thinks anyone he sees is going to hit him." The vet touched the dog's torn flesh quickly but gently, sponging it clean. "Rotten thing. Most people who hit dogs don't bring them to me, but I see them too often anyway."

Jones was almost to the door. Squeeze out through it and run until you can't run anymore, she told herself. It was the only plan she could think of.

"So then there's a dog thinks everyone is going to hit him. But not everyone hits dogs." She looked, then, at Jones, who was stuck in the doorway as though it were only inches wide. "You didn't." Then she said, "If you're brave, and you find the right person, they won't send you back to anyone who hurts you."

"Help Jones help good Jones good help," said the dog. He looked up at the vet and the vet nodded at him, as though she understood everything, though she couldn't possibly.

Jones was dismayed when she felt tears standing in her eyes, embarrassed when Dr. Kozlowski put a hand on her shoulder and walked her gently back inside. "It will help your friend," the vet said in a matter-of-fact way, "if you stroke his head so he knows he has a friend here while I'm sewing this up."

So that's what Jones did.

Fetish

In the aftermath of the affair I decide to grow a beard.

"Susan," my roommate Lelana says, warningly. Her skin is very dark and perfect; she would not risk its flawlessness. But she has seven tiny holes in her left ear. By day she wears seven small hoops of metal in them: copper, brass, bronze, pewter, silver, platinum and gold. When she dresses to go out seven gem studs spark her ear's rim: ruby, amber, topaz, emerald, sapphire, amethyst, and diamond. The diamond cost her two months' pay, and though she keeps it in a matchbox in the back of the tool drawer, she makes nervous remarks about burglars when she is not wearing it. A beard cannot be stolen.

I think about what it will look like. The tiny hairs I have plucked from under my chin are not light brown, but mahogany brown or translucent blonde or light red. I wonder what they might combine to be.

There is a body-modification studio near my two favorite used-book stores. None of its signs ever attracted me: Tattoos. Piercing. Scarification. Branding. The new sign says Body Hair, and it did not at first attract me either. I thought of legs and chests and the busboy at the coffee shop who has grown his arm hair thick as an orang-utan's, and dyed it orange red. He wears a blood-red tank top to show it off. I always look in my coffee cup for orange hairs which are never there.

I stand at the history shelf in the store next to the body studio and flip open a book on Egypt to a drawing of Cleopatra, her Pharoah's beard, a proud ruler's beard. It is not real. Not like mine. Like mine will be.

I stroke my chin.

Inside the studio are displays of jewelry, steel rings and chains, simple and in intricate combinations, stapled to framed swaths of black canvas. I don't know which parts of the body each piece is designed for. Perhaps a clever person can wear them anywhere. The woman behind the counter is talking to a young man. He is conservatively pierced, at least that I can see, two small silver hoops through one eyebrow. She has a pattern of scarification arching from the bridge of her nose across her temple, where it disappears in the wispy black hair over her left ear. I have lived in the city for six years now, and seen a thousand such alterations. It still looks odd to me.

"Yes?" she says, after the young man has written out a check and left.

"A beard," I say. When she opened her mouth I could see a silver stud in her tongue.

"Yes, what style are you interested in?" She lisps, just a little, enough to remind me not to look at her mouth. I look at her scar, a curlicue like an edge of paisley. If she didn't want me to look at it, she wouldn't have had it put there.

"What do you mean?"

"We'll stimulate the follicles wherever you want it," she says. Shtimulate. "You won't have to trim it like some man would, since you're starting out with nothing there at all. Where you don't have it added it won't make it grow." She gropes around under the counter and pulls out a small spiral-bound book, line drawings of strangely-shaped sideburns, fringes of hair like necklaces, Dali moustaches: facial hair in patterns of tufts, in lines and curves, I have never imagined.

"I don't know. Just a beard."

"Think about it. You can call for an appointment." She gives me a brochure, "Hair Growth and You." "We haven't had too many women yet for this. I think you should do it."

"Would you?" I ask her.

"Oh no, that's not me," she says. She traces her forefinger in a curl down her right cheek and up to the corner of her mouth. "I'm going to mark myself here, as soon as I get the pattern drawn up exactly right. Hair would cover it up."

Myshelf.

At home I read from the brochure to Lelana. She frowns at me but stops telling me to shut up after the third time. "'Within two days of topical Hirexidin application and regular intake of the supplemental hormones, most clients will find unstimulated fine body hairs falling out and new, thick hair taking its place.'"

"Who writes those things?" she asks. She's tried something new with her ear: four rings, three studs. I'm not used to seeing the diamond out of the bottom hole. She twists it, in its second position, between thumb and forefinger.

"It's fast," I say.

"It's a drug," she says. "Hormone. Thingie. Don't you need a doctor?"

"There's a doctor who prescribes it." His name is stamped in the blank space on the back of the brochure. "Then the person at the studio who applies it is a registered nurse. She does the branding and scarification, too. It's all very clean."

"Oh great," says Lelana. "Why are you doing this?"

The nurse has me sit back in a big old vinyl dentist's chair. Over its fake-leather maroon it has been spray-painted with gold and silver swirls.

She wears rubber gloves and holds a thin cloth patch. It has been traced already with the shape of my beard: larger than a goatee, but trim, with a moustache. When I told the receptionist I wanted a beard, not something abstract, she tried to talk me into leaving a blank design, my initials or a geometric space, in the middle. That's what the few fashionable women are wearing, but I don't want that.

The nurse takes a scissors and cuts carefully on the thin red ink lines until it looks like a construction-paper beard a child would put on with a string. Then she peels the adhesive from the patch. With her gloves, it takes her two false starts to peel it. I have washed my face thoroughly and wiped an astringent over it; my chin tingles. My breath feels tight in my chest as I wait for her to drape the patch over my face. Her movements are precise and careful. Where the patch clings to my skin I feel a heat, building slowly. I don't know if is the treatment or the excitement.

I have to wear the patch for twenty-four hours and go back to have things checked out. I have taken off work. I look at it in the mirror. It looks like a cheap Halloween costume. The patch is a light pink-tan color that looks like no one's skin ever did. It is darker than my own skin, so that, if I squint and blur my vision, it almost looks like a pale beard. Or like something is wrong with my skin.

It stings coming off. The nurse holds a moist strip of paper up against my twinging cheek. She looks at it. It is blue.
"Good," she says.

I have little white pills I'm supposed to take. In some way they direct testosterone to the follicles marked by the Hirexiden. They are so small they look like pills for a cat.

I swallow one with some orange juice and look in the mirror. My face looks the same as ever, but flushed, irritated, where the beard is supposed to come in. Makeup could smooth the color out, but the brochure says to clean the area gently and put no other products on it.

No one seems to look at me when I walk to the grocery store. I brush my fingers along the lower slopes of my cheeks. Has the peach fuzz fallen out, crowded out by more virile hairs? I can't tell. My fingertips seem too sensitive, they seem to have caught the tingling of my reddened cheeks. I pull at my chin, then stop, hoping I haven't disrupted anything.

I buy frozen burritos, pretzels, chocolate bars and more orange juice. I think the checkout clerk is staring at me, too polite to say anything. I smile at him.

o o o

I wake Tuesday with a definite stubble on my chin. Lelana narrows her eyes at me when we pass in the bathroom hall. I put on mascara and a little more eyeshadow than I normally use and go to work.

Everyone in the office is pretty conservative in their grooming. They have seen facial hair in the high-fashion magazines and on MTV, but fancy, not like mine. Gaze after gaze glances off my chin without a word spoken. I spend most of the day on the phone trying to track down a lost report. The receiver pushes against the stubble. The people on the other end of the line don't know it. I eat lunch outside, in the courtyard by the downtown sidewalks, watching pedestrians watching me, men almost frowning, women looking carefully bored.

Between bites, I rub the stubble with the back of my hand. If I kissed a man now he would be the one scratched, his cheeks as reddened as the back of my hand is reddened. Which of these men passing by would I kiss? They lower their eyes toward the sidewalk as they pass. I finish the sandwich I brought, two bags of chips, an apple, a banana and a bottle of beer, watching the men go by.

It's growing in thick and fast. I'm proud of it; I can hardly keep my hands off my face. The treatment, the hormones, they started it, but it's my follicles that have risen to the call, that are putting forth this rich growth, this life on my face.

Lelana's boyfriend comes over to pick her up Friday night and looks startled when I answer the door, the first open look of surprise I've seen. She must not have told him. She hurries past me and ushers him out of the apartment building. I sit through the afternoon watching arena football on cable. It's cute how they run around the small stadium wearing skintight uniforms bare up to the knee. After the game I watch two old black and white romance movies. I realize Lelana has come back in without my noticing only when I hear a sullen rattle of pots and pans in the kitchen. Two commercial breaks later, the door to her room shuts firmly.

I wake with my fingers buried in the short thick growth of my beard, and, comfortable, sleep again.

o o o

It's beautiful, all the colors I thought it might be, an autumn beard of brown and red and sparkles of blonde. I experiment with the best eye makeup to complement it. The sink is crowded with pencils and trays of powder and tiny tubs of cream in every color of brown, russet, charcoal. It is a month since I started growing the beard, and it is better than I ever hoped it would be. As I start to work on my face, I wonder idly where Lelana is. Around.

When I finish with my eyes I take a small scissors and carefully trim my beard until it is perfect.

I wear tight black pants and a clinging dark blue top, open in a small keyhole at the chest but with a turtleneck against which the beard glows. I shopped for the outfit for days. I brush my beard, I fluff it, I look at it from all angles in the mirror. I run my fingers quickly through my hair and go out the door.

Everyone looks at me at the club. Everyone.

I dance alone on the floor for an hour. For two hours. Then the men, tentatively at first, then in growing numbers, begin to crowd around me. I pick and choose from them. Too weedy, too loud, hair too limp. Finally I let one dance with me, slow, his breath warm and moist in my beard.

Lelana is not in the apartment when I take him home. I kiss the man and feel my beard catch on the angles of his smooth, naked cheeks, his lips. We do not need to talk. One hand tangled in my beard, the other on my breast, he lets me press him down against the bed. As he gasps, he pulls at my beard, pulls at my real and living beard.

When I send him home, I have not asked his name. I sleep with sweat and kisses in my beard and dream nothing at all.

In the morning, I shave.

Alita in the Air

A loud voice over the speakers said they were descending into Tuscon. Alita's ears started hurting. Sick with boredom, really quite sure you could throw up from boredom—that would be what the airsick bags were for—she tried to see if there was anything interesting out the airplane's window.

No, there wasn't.

And she thought about landing and all the bother and nonsense and Uncle Roy who was really boring too. Uncle Roy and the horrible forsaken desert and all of the summer there. And she thought of something mischievous to do when she got there.

But she didn't mean to do it really.

The plane landed with a bump and a jostle, pushing her head forward as they dragged to a halt down the runway. The seatbelt sign turned off with a ping after the plane had driven around for a while, by which time Alita had already unfastened her buckle. She stood up on her seat, her head hunched under the overhead baggage compartments, impatient for all the well-fed grownup bodies to get out of her way in the narrow aisle.

"Alita?" said the flight attendant, in the syrupy voice she hated. He was the one who had taken her from the check-in guy in Chicago, and held her hand like she was a baby, all the way down the aisle to her seat in back. He was the one who'd pinned the plastic airline wings over the picture of the Ferris wheel on her t-shirt, next to the sticker that said UNACCOMPANIED CHILD. The tag on his uniform said JERRY and she didn't like him any better than anyone else.

"We'll just be waiting for the other passengers to leave the plane. Then I'll take you up to meet your uncle," Jerry said sweetly. Alita nodded and fingered the plastic souvenir pin and hated Arizona. Just looking out the window at the low airport buildings shimmering in the sun made her hate it.

Arizona was so bad it was worse than being on a stupid airplane, she was sure. At least on an airplane they mostly left you alone. Uncle Roy had been on the phone with her mother for an hour and all the plans for the next month were disgusting.

"Okay time to go," Jerry said like it was one word. He put his hand out. Alita looked away from it. He grabbed her hand and genially hustled her down the plane's aisle. "So you're vacationing in Tucson? That's just great. What are you going to do?"

"Nothing," Alita said.

"That's just great," Jerry said, dragging her down the aisle and into the jetway that connected the plane to the airport building.

Great, Alita thought. Just great. There was a blast of hot air, where the jetway joined to the building, that made her shiver. Great. The building was air-conditioned, but surrounded by Arizona. Uncle Roy would probably want to go right out iguana-hunting, or whatever they did in Arizona.

"I have Alita here," Jerry said to the woman at the check-in podium. He handed her the papers Alita's mother had given to the man at the podium in Chicago.

The podium woman's nametag said CHARLOTTE. "Well let's see who we've got here," Charlotte said, smiling, in the same syrupy one-word rush Jerry talked in. Alita scowled. A man came forward from the crowd, bald, and smiling too.

"Hi, Alita!" said Uncle Roy. He was holding a pink teddy bear for cripe's sake.

So she did it, the mischief she had thought of on the airplane.

"Who are you?" she said to Uncle Roy.

"What?" said Uncle Roy.

"What?" said Charlotte, her dumb talk-to-the-kid smile fading. "Honey, isn't this the person who's supposed to meet you?"

"I never saw him," Alita said. She raised her voice. "My Uncle Roy is supposed to meet me."

"I'm Roy Mahaffey," Uncle Roy said.

"Isn't this your Uncle Roy?" Charlotte said, and "Uncle Roy has black hair and he's taller," said Alita, at the same time. This could work. She fingered the stupid UNACCOMPANIED CHILD sticker and widened her eyes to look like a very kidnapable kid.

"Alita, you remember me," Uncle Roy said.

"I want my Uncle Roy," Alita said.

"Sir, could I see some ID?" Charlotte said.

"This is crazy," said Uncle Roy, digging in his pocket.

"I want my Uncle Roy!" Alita said. She wondered if she was play-ing it too hard. But grownup strangers never did seem to know the difference between a twelve-year-old and a kid of five or six.

"It's the right address. Sir, what's your phone number?" Charlotte was peering at Uncle Roy's driver's license and at the forms that Jerry had brought from the plane with Alita.

"Look, even on the driver's license he doesn't have black hair like my Uncle Roy! It's a fake!" Alita said.

"What's wrong with you?" Uncle Roy said, reaching out to touch her arm.

Alita shrieked and jumped behind Charlotte. Uncle Roy looked baffled. Alita grabbed Charlotte's sleeve. She had to stretch her eyes wide to keep from laughing.

Charlotte shuffled some papers and called a supervisor and for a while there were a lot of people standing around, and finally they told Uncle Roy that if he left they wouldn't call the police.

"But I never had black hair, and you know who I am! I bought you that book for Christmas," he said to Alita. Alita made a show of looking away from him. It had been a stupid book anyway.

Uncle Roy walked away slowly, hunching his shoulders, the pink teddy bear dangling in his loose grip.

"Now what?" Alita asked Charlotte. She was feeling cheerful. The first part of it had been kind of embarrassing, lying such a big lie, but once she got used to it, it was exciting, making the grownups jump. Anyway Uncle Roy wasn't even in trouble. He'd left before anyone called the police.

"Now," said Charlotte. She pressed her lips together, which made her look less like an airline person and more like Alita's mother when she was tired and angry. Which was how Alita's mother looked most of the time lately.

"–Now we'll put her back on a plane home," said Charlotte's supervisor, who was so important he didn't have a name on a tag. "And since this one is turning around in another forty minutes, we should get her back on it now. Call an attendant."

The supervisor wrote on a lot of papers and gave them to the new flight attendant, whose nametag said MIMI. Mimi smiled briefly at Alita and hauled her by the hand back into the jetway. The hot air blasted them again where the jetway attached, and Alita felt very clever to have avoided the whole trauma of a summer in the desert.

On the way back, Alita watched the sky turn red and purple with sunset until it was mostly black, then pulled down the plastic windowshade.

The flight attendant gave her a headset for free, which was good because the one she'd paid for on the way to Arizona had taken a big chunk of her pocket money. It was another movie her mother wouldn't let her see in a movie theater, full of people shooting and kissing.

It was a boring movie, on a little television screen hanging from the ceiling, partly blocked by a passenger's bald head. Dinner was served just as Alita was getting sick of it, something with noodles that stuck to the plastic tray and a measly cookie for dessert. Alita finished eating the cookie, took off the headphones and played Game Boy.

About the time she reached level 17 of Rajah Princess, she started to think about what she could say to her mother when she landed.

"Uncle Roy wasn't there," she'd say. *He was there, Alita,* she imagined her mother saying. "No, no, no! A kidnapper pretending to be Uncle Roy was there." In her mind, Alita's mother shook her head angrily. *Haven't you heard of the telephone, Alita? Uncle Roy called me and told me all about it.*

Alita swallowed. "It didn't look like Uncle Roy," she told her mother in her head," and "Actually nobody showed up at all–

Uncle Roy must have been telling you a story so he wouldn't get in trouble," and "He told me he was a kidnapper!" In her mind, her mother frowned harder and harder.

The plane landed before she could think of anything that wouldn't make her mother frown. "Okay time to go," Mimi said, like it was one word, and clamped a hand around Alita's wrist and pulled her out into the jetway to the O'Hare airport building. The air that came through there was pretty hot, too, and muggy. "They called your mother from Tucson, so she should be here."

When Alita saw her mother, standing there with Marsh-mouth at her hip and frowning just like Alita had imagined, she could only think of one thing to say.

"That's not my mother," she whispered to the man at the podium, ALFRED.

"What?" said Alfred, and "Alita Matilda Anderson!" said her mother. Alfred looked at her.

Nothing for it:

"That proves it's not my mother," Alita said. "She guessed my middle name wrong."

Her mother was frowning very hard.

"Matilda Brunhilda what a pill-da," said Marsh.

"It's not Matilda, it's—" She got on tiptoes and whispered into Alfred's ear. "Mimi," she whispered. "See if she can guess that!"

Alfred pursed his lips and looked through all the papers. "It just says Alita M. Anderson here," he said.

"I know my own name," Alita said. "The international *kidnapping* conspiracy doesn't."

"What's the child's middle name?" Alfred asked her mother.

"Also I don't live here," she whispered to Alfred. "My dad lives in California, but he's moving to New York, and he sent me to Chicago to visit my grandma while we move. Does she look old enough to be my grandma?"

"Middle name?" Alfred repeated.

"Oh for pete's— Young lady, when I get you home!" Alita's mother said. Alita cried, "Don't let her steal me!"

"Can you tell me the name?" Alfred said.

"I never—it's Matilda. After her great-grandmother."

Alita always hated that name. "No," she said.

"I'm not going to play this game," her mother said. She looked at Alfred and he looked at her. She turned red.

"Myrtle," she said. "Meredith. Megan. Margerie. Mehitabel. For pete's sake!"

"I don't know this stupid girl either," Marsh said. Alita glared at him, changed her mind, and smiled sweetly. Imagine not having to share with Marsh-mouth anymore. Marsh had on his most innocent face, the one he used to tell their mother whoppers about Alita.

"She said she was going to get another kid because I didn't scrub the floors fast enough," Marsh said loudly.

"Young man!" their mother said. Her voice was as loud as pots and pans smashing against a wall. Alita had seen her angry hundreds of times since Alita's father had moved away to wherever he'd really gone—no one ever told her where—but this was the most ever. The plan had better work, or she was sure to be cooked.

"And do the laundry and peel the vegetables and mow the lawn and wax the car and—"

"Don't let her take me for child labor!" Alita said. Marsh was pretty clever, really, for a stupid kid.

Then Alfred called his supervisor, and there was a lot of fuss and noise and Alita was the center of everyone's attention again. Alita's mother turned redder and redder yet. Finally she picked Marsh right up off the floor—his canvas sneakers kicking ten inches in the air—and said, "Make your bed and lie in it, young lady," and turned on her heel. Alita watched them leave, Marsh dangling in their mother's grip, but not forgetting to stick his tongue out at her goodbye.

Victory! By the time she decided to come home, her mother would be sorry.

"Now what?" she said cheerfully to Alfred and his supervisor and all the grownups crowded around.

They looked at each other.

"There's a red-eye flight to Portland," Alfred said.

He typed a lot on his computer and the supervisor filled out some forms and Alita got put on a cart which whizzed her across the airport to a different terminal, where RAMON took her by the wrist and hustled her onto another airplane. There were very few people on it, mostly businessmen sleeping with their jackets laid out, like blankets with arms, across their chests.

Alita was sort of hungry, but all Ramon gave out to eat was pretzels, so she drank a lot of cola and stayed up all night. No one cared if she went to sleep. That was fun for a while, but the plane didn't have a movie and there was no rap on the music channels and the left earpiece on the earphones didn't make any sound.

Still, she could play Game Boy way past anyone's bedtime.

Rajah Princess wasn't as hard in the little-screen version, and she didn't have her other cartridges. They were in her purse. Her purse was gone. She pushed the call button for Ramon and told him. He shrugged. "It's probably in Chicago," he said, hurrying off to answer another call.

The sun was coming up when they landed in Portland. Ramon pulled her down the aisle to the terminal building, where SYDNEY looked at her papers and put her on a plane to San Diego. Alita was very tired, but a baby was crying in the seat behind her, and she couldn't sleep. She asked the flight attendant, MARY-SUE, if she could move seats. "The plane is full," Mary-Sue told her shortly, and handed her a cold mushroom omelette. An hour and a half later, Mary-Sue grabbed Alita's hand and hustled her out to meet BOB at the podium.

Bob wrote some things on her papers and sent her to the gate right next door. Alita's stomach hurt and her eyes felt like they were full of sand. It was hard to shut them and hard to keep them open.

She nearly fell asleep in an airport chair anyway, but then WENDY had her wrist in an iron grip and was dragging her off. Wendy plopped Alita down in a seat between a fat businessman and a fat guy in a baseball hat and a smelly t-shirt. They both ordered a lot of drinks and told loud awful jokes to each other over Alita's head the whole way to Newark. Alita got out her Game Boy and tried to ignore them.

The battery died just about the time the pilot told everyone over the speakers that they were crossing the Mississippi. Alita groaned. She put the blanket over her head and tried to sleep. Maybe she slept, but if she did, she dreamed the guffaws of two large men all the way through it.

"Not another one of these," said PAT in Newark. He tapped on his computer and wrote some things on the papers and sent Alita right back on the same airplane, this time with GEOFFREY.

"Can I get some batteries somewhere?" Alita asked Geoffrey.

"We don't keep batteries on the airplane," Geoffrey said. He gave her a pack of playing cards with pictures of vodka bottles and the airline's name on them. No good solitaire game fit on a little airplane tray.

Alita flew to Minneapolis, and San Francisco, and Houston, and Jacksonville. It was probably on the Houston flight that she misplaced the dead Game Boy. From Jacksonville she took a bunch of little hops up the East Coast, up to Boston. By Boston her hair felt really greasy, and there were stains on her t-shirt.

"I want to go home now," she told BERNICE.

"Home would be California, or would it be New York?" said Berenice, peering at her papers through glasses that had a chain behind them. "No, wait: Tucson?"

"Aurora, Illinois," Alita said, trying to comb her hair smooth with her fingers. Her brush had been in her purse.

"Portland?" said Berenice.

"It's near Chicago," Alita said.

"I don't have any records of that," said Berenice. "We'll put you on a plane to Boise."

"Can I have a bath?" Alita said. She was exhausted.

Berenice handed her off to JOE, who put her on a seat near the bathroom, which had a long line to it as soon as the seatbelt sign went off. Finally Alita went in and tried to wash her hair in the tiny little sink, using liquid soap from the pump. She got water all over her t-shirt. The ink ran on the UNACCOMPANIED CHILD sticker.

Joe tsk'd and got her another sticker. "We have to follow procedure," he said.

"I want to go home now," Alita said. Joe handed her a bag of sugar-coated peanuts and didn't stop by her seat for the rest of the flight.

She flew to Seattle and Fresno and Las Vegas and Atlanta. She ripped her t-shirt in Atlanta and HOLLY gave her a new one with the airline's logo on it. It was too big even to be baggy. It might as well have been a nightgown.

She tried to use the airplane phone to call her mother. The phone needed a credit card to work. She tried to get to an airport phone, but MICHELLE held on to her wrist at the gate in St. Louis, and RANDY kept his hand clamped on her shoulder in Cleveland, and JOHN made her sit in an airport chair and didn't take his eyes off her until they were ready to board in El Paso.

When they did announce it was time to preboard unaccompanied minors in El Paso, Alita made a break for the phone banks. John was much faster than she was and she was hustled on the plane before she had a chance to protest.

And after that, they kept her on the plane after everyone else had disembarked. If the plane was going on to somewhere else, she stayed in her seat. If it wasn't, she sat on the plane watching the cleaning people put the magazines back into the magazine bin and throw out people's crumpled tissues, until another plane was ready and KATHERINE or PHIL or GREGORY escorted her to it.

But she never was on the ground very much. Most of the time she was high above the earth, flying through clouds and sunshine and rain and peering down, in the middle of the night, at thousands of tiny lights that were each someone's house, snug and firmly on the ground.

She never seemed to be able to sleep.

She was always too cold.

The airplane food was awful.

The seats were lumpy, and the other seats pressed in so close all around her it felt hard to breathe.

On long flights, she would slip her seatbelt off when the fasten-seatbelts sign went off, and stand in the tiny galley at the back of the airplane by the bathrooms. That was the nearest thing to breathing space on an airplane, but you couldn't be there more than a minute or two without being in someone's way. Passengers would jostle past her on their way to one of the bathrooms.

"Excuse me," Alita said until the words came out automatically without her thinking about them. Sometimes the passenger was a kid, who'd look at her curiously, and try to strike up a conversation about where she was flying to. For a while she avoided kids, then for a while she told whoppers about the trip to Paris or India she'd just come from or was on her way to, and then it made her sick have to talk about where she could be instead of on an airplane, and she avoided kids again.

Even more than with the passengers, she was in the way of the flight attendants trying to use the gallery. It was JOYCE and BILL trundling the heavy metal meal cart by, as Alita pulled her toes out of the way of its wheels, or GUNTHER reaching around her to turn on the coffeemaker, or CAROL sliding empty food trays into a cabinet rack on the back wall of the airplane, or FAY dashing to get club soda and a napkin for a woman who'd squirted mustard on her blouse.

The flight attendants were always moving, rushing around the narrow spaces of the airplane doing everything. They paid no attention to Alita anymore when they weren't moving her from one plane to another, so she could squeeze herself into a corner—never out of the way for very long, someone always needed something from wherever you could stow yourself—and watch them and listen. The flight attendants smiled at passengers and sighed when their backs were turned. They pushed stray hair back behind their ears, took deep breaths, and hurried off to answer calls. When they thought no one was looking, they leaned heavily on the steel gallery countertop with their eyes shut. Just for a moment: then they would put on bright expressions again and pour someone some orange juice. Alita, part of the airplane furniture, saw such things the passengers didn't, and kept them to herself.

One night, on a red-eye from Detroit to Oakland, LILLIAN leaned over her and tucked the thin airline blanket up under Alita's chin. It was the nicest thing anyone had done in a very long time. Alita whispered, her eyes hot and squeezed shut, "Can't I go home?"

The woman murmured so softly Alita could barely hear her. "What home?" Alita kept her eyes shut and strained to hear over the rush of the airplane's jets. "Look out the window: a million little lights. A million little houses. Do you belong to any of them?"

"But I have to belong somewhere," Alita whispered.

"How long have you been flying, Alita? No one down there knows where you are. Where do you think you belong now?"

Alita shuddered and opened her eyes. Lillian was three rows ahead, pouring a drink for a skinny woman in a pink suit. The flight attendant's face was a polite blank, but when she turned and glanced at Alita there was exhausted sympathy on her face.

Alita shut her eyes again and slept fitfully. She dreamed a half-awake dream of the airplane flying thousands and thousands and thousands of miles away from the earth, until the earth was a twinkling little light out the window indistinguishable from all the others. When she opened her eyes and looked outside, she was confused whether she was looking down at distant homes or distant planets.

Her hurting ears let her know they were descending into Orange County. When the grownups and their Accompanied Children had all filed off the plane, Alita stood up, feeling stiff and sore all over. The cleaning crew was getting on the plane.

Without a word, Alita took a trash bag from one of the woman and started to pick up little pieces of paper and junk the passengers had dropped on the floor.

Lillian stood by the door to the jetway, talking to the pilot. When

Alita caught her eye, Lillian smiled and nodded, and the pilot did, too.

They finished cleaning the plane, the cleaning crew and Alita, and Lillian took Alita's wrist and hustled her out saying "You have a nice time okay?" like any flight attendant, and handed her off to SOPHIE who put Alita on a plane to Dallas/Fort Worth.

Many months later Alita landed in Chicago, and after she'd cleaned the plane and helped with the baggage and was being taken to a gate for Boise, she looked and looked for her mother or even Marsh, but all the smiling faces belonged to strangers.

Now she looked forward to landings. When the passengers were gone, she could vacuum and change toilet-paper rolls and do something besides pretend to be a passenger herself. She wasn't a passenger.

One day, when she had worn out another airline t-shirt and her jeans were too snug around the hips, PATRICIA and JO gave her, instead of another shirt and pants, a wheeled carry-on suitcase like the ones the flight attendants all used. Alita looked at it and looked at them: they looked silently back at her. She unzipped the case. Inside it was a navy-blue skirted suit and a striped blouse, identical to theirs.

Wordlessly, she took them into the bathroom. There, with the efficiency she'd learned from a thousand hours in that minute space, she stripped off her old life, the worn-out kid's t-shirt and jeans, stuffed it all in the little trash chute, and put on her new one.

A hundred flights later, an UNACCOMPANIED CHILD of thirteen or so named Marshall, half a foot taller than the last time she'd seen him but still shorter than the young woman she was, got on the airplane in Chicago.

"So you're going to have a summer vacation in Tucson how nice," ALITA said in one sugary practiced breath as she pulled him by the wrist through the jetway, and "You have a nice time okay now?" she said a few hours later as she left him with the gate attendant.

And, when he turned and looked at her, frowning a little, she smiled a perfect flight-attendant's smile and said, "And behave yourself."

Then Alita went back home onto the airplane.

To Destroy Rats

This is the only way to destroy rats.

I have lived with mice, in a sort of tolerant hatred, or hateful tolerance. I have laid traps for them, and they have laughed at the traps. In the night I could hear them whisper to each other, almost catch the mousely details of their plans for snatching bits of cheese, or even smears of peanut butter, from the fateful lever, the one meant to trip death down onto their necks. I could hear them giggle as it fed them instead.

Hateful, fateful: mice love rhymes, love all manner of trivial foolish games; mice put these idiot rhymes into my head. That is another reason I do not like mice. But I can live with this inanity. Mice are fools with their foolish games, and the best they can hope for is stalemate, petty irritation, which I, man to their rodent, am evolved past regarding.

Rats make war. It is rats or you, you or rats. Rats will win by any means necessary. You must fight by any means necessary.

I must win by any means.

First I tried the things they suggest, those hardware-store men who do not know war except as a field for commerce. I tried the bigger, crueler, rat-sized cousin of the spring traps the mice had giggled at. The rats relieved them of their treats and temptations, quietly, guerrillas stealing in and out of battle before their enemy—I—could see them, not a blur of visible movement, not a whisper of noise.

I poisoned the bait, and with hideous rattish intelligence they let the poison be. I bought catch-ems promised by the hardware men to stick and pull their cunning, ugly hands and feet, and in the morning I would look for the baleful stare of an immobilized rodent that never was there. A rat knows the difference between the careless bounties of man, and his lies. Rats do not joke and do not giggle, but somewhere hidden in my walls they mocked me.

Before I had attained the will necessary to ignore the mice, I once purchased a cat, for five dollars, from a banal little housewife down the street, reasoning that suffering the intrusion of one alien creature in my house would be more tolerable than the presence of dozens of chattering, asinine little rodents. The cat was plump and white, with blank blue eyes, bearing some grotesque name—Fluffy or Muffins—that I dismissed as soon as the silly woman pronounced it to me, along with her protestations that she would have pampered the creature until its eventual death of obese old age had her snot-nosed daughter not developed an allergy.

After I had brought it in its carry-case to my home, and told it to earn its keep with slaughter, I had soon learned it was no more than vermin itself. The creature would sit at the foot of my chair or my bed, staring as though it expected something of me. Feed yourself, I told it.

But it had refused. Though fat mice scampered through the walls, the hapless brute expected to feed off me just as they did: yet with the gall to demand I cater to it willingly. Its presence became more insistent, as though this were its house, not mine. It stared at me hour after hour. Intolerable. Finally I had been compelled to shove the scrawny thing back into its carry-case, using a broom I later discarded, and take it out to a scrubby little wood miles from my house.

There is no good in this mendicity, I told it, when it refused to come out of the case and find its way in the woods. You are a man, beholden to no one, or you are vermin. And I walked away, knowing I might have to live with mice, but at least I would never again share my home with anything that selfishly presumptuous. Mice, at least, behind their bravado, are cowards.

But I had not then calculated on rats.

The mice had taken little notice of this feline incursion. Only the arrival of the rats drove them off. After the rats came, I never heard another giggle. The mice knew which was the real threat.

o o o

To destroy rats, it would take much sterner measures than those that had already failed against mice.

I purchased guns. I sat in the kitchen late one night, the next night, the next night, the next. I slept days, calling in sick, because rats are patient and can wait one night, two, or three. On the fifth night one walked calmly in front of the stove. I could hear its claws click on the linoleum. Slowly I raised the barrel of my nine-millimeter pistol. The creature stopped in its path and looked at me. It was nearly the size of my two fists, its eye calmly baleful. I centered my aim on its dark and scruffy body and squeezed the trigger. The noise deafened me and it was some moments before I looked for the fragments of its corpse. What I saw was a sharp black hole in the broiler door of the oven. The rat was gone.

Over the next three nights they came and went as they pleased through the kitchen. Foam plugs in my ears, I fired at every shadow of their movement. My hand is steady and my eye good, but I killed not one of them. The third night the officers came to my door, and after I finally managed to send them away, the smaller of the two darting a suspicious look back at me, I unloaded the clips from the guns. Defending one's home against intruders should not fairly attract the attention of the law, but there it was.

The rats would accept a victory won that way, though it was not of their own merit, the dishonorable cheaters, but I would not give it to them. This war is man against creature: they take me down or I take them. I would not let them make allies of my fellow man. I shut the guns away in the closet.

I put the brightest lights in every socket, floodlights in the single-outlet ceiling fixtures and 150-watt incandescent bulbs in the multiple-socket chandeliers, and left them on all night and all day. I bought lamps, and armed them, likewise, with 150-watt bulbs. I wore sunglasses; I slept, by day, with a black cloth tied around my eyes. Even with dark glasses the light was staggering. I found myself stumbling on a simple walk to the bathroom. This torture would surely drive them, screaming, to thrash helplessly on my floors. Behind the wallboards was the dark they craved, but if they stayed there they would starve. And they could not leave.

And yet. I would grope my way through the overheated, over-bright air of my house to a cupboard to take down a box of cereal, and find new holes gnawed through the cardboard box and plastic interior bag. Deposited beside spilled crumbs of flaked wheat were several hard dark turds, the carelessly confident signature of an insolent parasite.

What were they doing? Squeezing their beady eyes tight against radiation and navigating my home by cunning memory? I tried to find out but could not see their passage in the blinding electrical glare. They had turned my offensive to their own advantage, again.

If I could not starve them out indirectly I must do so directly. I removed every bit of food from the kitchen. I ate pizza and Chinese food that I had delivered to my door, wrapped the remains in plastic and drove them by night to deposit in back-alley dumpsters half a mile from my house.

The rats did not leave. I could hear them. Turds began to appear in the middle of the floor, where, horribly, before I learned to look, I stepped, slipped, on them. By my bed, in the hallway, in the center of the bathtub. Insolence.

I scrubbed the kitchen down. Not a dried spill of orange juice down a cupboard, not a crumb of toast remained. I ran the vacuum cleaner for hours. There was no place in my house that could not be used to perform surgery.

Except that there was still the spoor of the rats, trailing across my path.

There was no mirth in their joke: there was dead serious purpose. They announced themselves masters of my human domain; they would settle for nothing now but my total defeat, my total acquiescence. It was written in the toothmarks they left nibbled on the legs of my furniture. In rattish code these marks demanded surrender. Though I had not fully seen one since the rat who evaded my first bullet, their takeover of my house was thorough and unmerciful. I had failed to destroy them.

How could I destroy them? Rats are not prey for humans, but their unwelcome beneficiaries. Before there were humans, rats scraped a miserable existence, forced to compete among a hundred honest beasts. When man appeared, the rats rejoiced. Human civilization was the making of them. It would be justice to tear civilization down, if only to spite their lazy, criminal triumph.

Thinking that, I sat in my kitchen, a room cold and bright and sterile, but still the playground of vermin. There was no visible hint they were there, or that the mice they had driven away with their bullying muscle had been there before. But I could feel their presence. I knew they were now so bold as to walk through every room of my house, just outside the edges of my vision; but the kitchen, empty as it was of food, remained their stronghold. I sat in my kitchen with a lighter and a candle and the last two weeks of morning newspaper, bundled neatly in a paper shopping bag. That neatness was marred. They had shredded and stolen paper from one corner. Somewhere it was made into a nest, for hideous pink naked rat infants to squall in.

I flicked the lighter on and off. I lit the candle and held it to the bag. An inch away; closer. I turned off the light switch and moved the candle again, watched the torn newspaper glow by orange flame. If I burned down the house they would die, roasted between the wallboards, shrunken charcoal corpses. Firemen's hoses would wash them, crumbling, into the gutters.

I touched the flame to the bag. I could feel tiny eyes staring at me. Then I knew that they were in no danger from the fire, that they were already deserting, as rats always desert. The flames would not outrun them. They would watch the fire from the bushes in the back of the yard, and when the ashes cooled, they would return to steal final spoils from the ruins.

Yellow flame licked from the shredded newspaper. I stamped it out. Even man's first and deadliest tool means nothing to rats. Blackened ripples in beige linoleum remained as witness to a last rodent victory.

As long as man walks the earth, the parasite rat will prey on the fruits of his labor. To destroy rats I would have to destroy every human artifact. That is out of my power.

Yet this is war. To quit is to surrender, to surrender is to be enslaved.

The chemical stench from the bubbled linoleum wafts around me. I can feel them peering around cabinets and appliances, looking to see what has become of my fire. Disappointed, no doubt, that I have not finished the job, failed to burn myself homeless or burn myself up, while they simply moved to the next house down the block. One less man, two dozen more rats.

I can hear them scuttling restlessly. I think I see a whisker twitch. They are all around me, wondering what I will do next, what pathetic failed attempt it will be. Their stubborn insistence on life at any price now teaches me that animals indeed have more vital force than we do. I thought I had invested everything in this war, but they had more to give than I did. In this moment I nearly give in to despair. I did everything the human mind can devise, and their sheer animal persistence defeated me.

I nearly give it up, but instead I give it over.

No human effort can touch them. Their animal world is too small, pervasive, vital. I cannot reach down from my lofty world and point destruction at them.

Only in their animal world can they be caught and rent and killed, yet in that world there is not the matching hatred of my human soul. Only a human's soul can match a rat's for hatred. Only human hatred and animal hunger together could match their hatred and hunger. To kill any one of them would be worth any price. The hunger to kill rats grows. It consumes me. I follow the hunger where it leads.

I must be smaller to follow them when they run from me. I must be agile to turn their corners. I must smell them. I must hear them. I push my broad face into a hunter's point, a carnivorous spearhead. I pull my ears high, high to hear their rancid breathing. I open the pupils of my eyes high until no darkness could hide a rat from my sight. I bend my legs to springs. I curl my hands to claws. I am tooth and nail. I hear them running in all directions. They are too late.

I am destruction.

The cat tears at the confining cloth, tangling sleeves, and fur-catching zippers, until it is free, leaping with one fluid motion behind the refrigerator.

For hours there are strange sounds, hisses, growls, and high, tiny screams, from basement to attic.

Eventually the authorities declare the house abandoned.

The Arbitrary Placement of Walls

When it is put up for sale and the buyers' contractor inspects it, he says that, except for the bullet holes in the kitchen, it is the cleanest property he has examined in years.